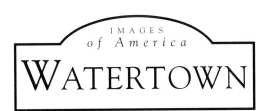

IMAGES
of America

WATERTOWN

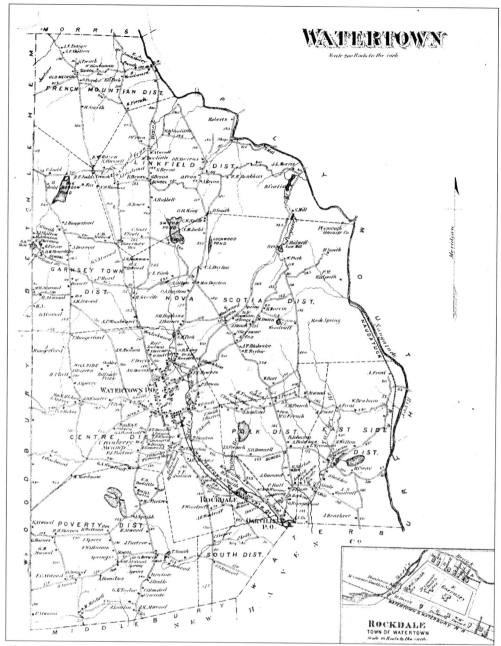

This 1859 map shows the nine school districts in Watertown. They were Centre, Linkfield, Nova Scotia, South, Polk, Garnseytown, East Side, French Mountain, and Poverty (later called Winnamaug). There were two rooms in the Centre School and one room in each of the others.

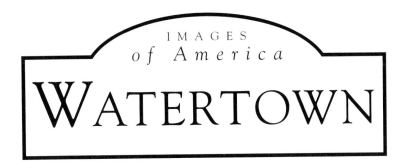

IMAGES
of America

WATERTOWN

Florence T. Crowell
Florence T. Crowell

ARCADIA

Published by Arcadia Publishing,
an imprint of Tempus Publishing, Inc.
2A Cumberland Street
Charleston, SC 29401

Printed in Great Britain.

Library of Congress Catalog Card Number: 2002101972

For all general information contact Arcadia Publishing at:
Telephone 843-853-2070
Fax 843-853-0044
E-Mail sales@arcadiapublishing.com

For customer service and orders:
Toll-Free 1-888-313-2665

Visit us on the internet at http://www.arcadiapublishing.com

*To my husband, Livingston, who has encouraged and supported
me in my many endeavors, and to my children, Julie, Betsy, John,
and Charles, who have shown patience and understanding as
I pursued my lifelong interest in history.*

CONTENTS

ACKNOWLEDGMENTS

Through the years, many people have shared their photographs, postcards, and memorabilia with the Watertown Historical Society. Much historical information has been collected that will be preserved for future generations. I would like to thank Jeffrey Grenier, president, and the society for giving me permission to use the photographs in the museum. I would also like to thank the following people for allowing me to use their photographs and for their support: Marge Hard Peircey, George McCleary, Anne Romano, Herbert King, William and Eleanor Quigley, J. William Hosking, Virginia Black Deitz, Charlie Crowell, Ruth Getsinger, Hobart Van Deusen, Sterling Goodwin, and Barbara Blum.

INTRODUCTION

Having been involved in local historical research as historical society president and vice president for more than 20 years, town historian for 13 years, and contributing writer for several local papers for more than 30 years, I am able to offer you this collection of images of Watertown, Connecticut. I have been fortunate to know some of Watertown's older residents and have gleaned from them much history of bygone days. They willingly shared their memories and photographs, which bring together the history of the town as it evolved when religious groups, early settlers, farmers, and blacksmiths moved to the area. Watertown was later able to enter the 20th century with the arrival of the train, the trolley, and the automobile. I want to pass on a history of a town that I have called home for the past 58 years. I hope you enjoy seeing these old photographs of Watertown from the 1800s to the 1950s.

The area of Connecticut that became Watertown, when it was incorporated in 1780, has an interesting history. In the 1680s, settlers who had moved from Farmington to Mattatuck, which was later called Waterbury, were attracted to the area by the fertile farmland and its many streams. They purchased a large tract of land from the Paugasett Indians. Farms and sawmills sprang up, and soon the people saw the need of a place of worship.

They petitioned the General Assembly in 1732, seeking permission to establish a parish and build a church because it was difficult for many to travel to the church in Waterbury. The first petition was rejected, and two more were necessary before permission to hire a preacher was granted in 1739. Independence from Waterbury was not granted until the Society of Westbury incorporated in 1780 and became Watertown. The First Ecclesiastical Society was formed, and services were held in the home of George Lewis. In January 1740, John Trumbull, a Yale graduate, was ordained pastor of the new parish. Plans were laid to build a meetinghouse in the corner of the cemetery. The building was completed in 1841, and the 300 residents belonged to one church.

The town was made up of farms, sawmills, gristmills, and homes. Fulling and carding mills followed, and in the early 1800s, pewter buttons were being made. Using waterpower, factories sprang up along the banks of Steele Brook. Through the years, Watertown became a farming community. There have been more than 30 dairy farms, and every farm had a flock of sheep. The sheep were sheared and the housewife spun the wool into yarn to make garments for the family.

In the middle of the 19th century, Watertown had started manufacturing items that were shipped worldwide. The Wheeler Wilson Sewing Machine Company produced the lock-stitch machine. Merrit Heminway and Sons was the first to wind silk thread on spools. When Heminway died, his son, Buel, and William Bartlett formed the Heminway and Bartlett Silk Company and continued to carry on the business. During World War II, the company made nylon thread and supplied parachute cord to the military. The Watertown Manufacturing Company incorporated in 1915 and, in the 1940s, manufactured melamine dinnerware for various branches of the service in World War II. In the late 1940s, the company made Lifetime Ware, a plastic dinnerware designed by Jon Hedu. This product was used in many homes in Watertown. The Oakville Pin Company made straight pins, safety pins, hooks, and snaps and employed hundreds of local residents. Seymour Smith and Sons purchased the old sewing machine factory and made bull rings, pruning shears, saws, and other garden tools.

As Watertown has grown, it has become difficult to visualize what it was like in the days of John Trumbull. Perhaps this book will allow the reader to catch a glimpse of the Watertown of yesteryear as we continue to grow and flourish in the 21st century.

One
WESTBURY BECOMES
WATERTOWN

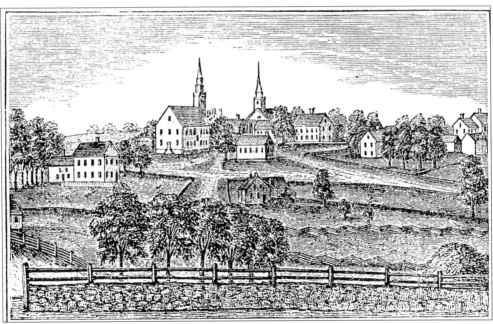

This is the earliest available sketch of the buildings in Watertown. Known as Westbury in 1739, the town was renamed when it was incorporated in 1780. In 1834 and 1835, John Warner Barber visited every town in the state and sketched several sites. In 1836, he published *Connecticut Historical Collections*. The building on the left is the second Congregational church, built in 1772 on the present-day site of the town hall. The other spire is the second Episcopal church, built in 1794 on the green. In 1772, Rev. John Trumbull, minister of the Congregational church, built the large house to the right of the churches. The small building in the foreground was a school that was built *c.* 1800 on the site of the first school.

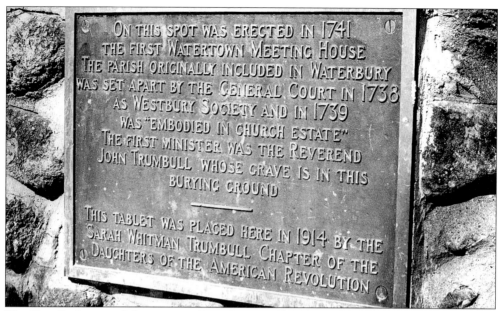

ON THIS SPOT WAS ERECTED IN 1741
THE FIRST WATERTOWN MEETING HOUSE
THE PARISH ORIGINALLY INCLUDED IN WATERBURY
WAS SET APART BY THE GENERAL COURT IN 1738
AS WESTBURY SOCIETY AND IN 1739
WAS "EMBODIED IN CHURCH ESTATE"
THE FIRST MINISTER WAS THE REVEREND
JOHN TRUMBULL WHOSE GRAVE IS IN THIS
BURYING GROUND

THIS TABLET WAS PLACED HERE IN 1914 BY THE
SARAH WHITMAN TRUMBULL CHAPTER OF THE
DAUGHTERS OF THE AMERICAN REVOLUTION

The First Ecclesiastical Society was formed in Westbury in May 1739. The next year, John Trumbull was ordained pastor of the new parish, and a meetinghouse was erected in the corner of the cemetery on Main Street. The building was demolished in 1732, and in 1914, the Daughters of the American Revolution placed this plaque in the stone wall at the corner of Main and French Streets.

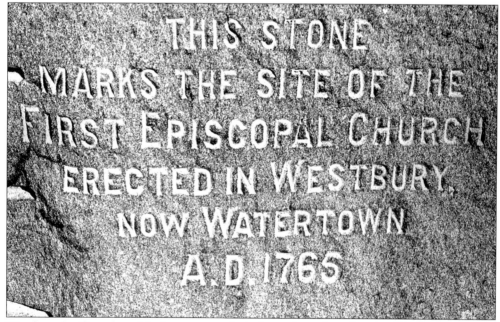

THIS STONE MARKS THE SITE OF THE FIRST EPISCOPAL CHURCH ERECTED IN WESTBURY, NOW WATERTOWN A.D. 1765

Westbury families who wished to pattern their form of worship after the Church of England built the first Episcopal church on the southeast corner of Main and French Streets. The building was taken down in 1794, when the new church was built on the green. This marker, erected by Mr. and Mrs. Heminway, was recently incorporated into the wall at the beginning of French Street

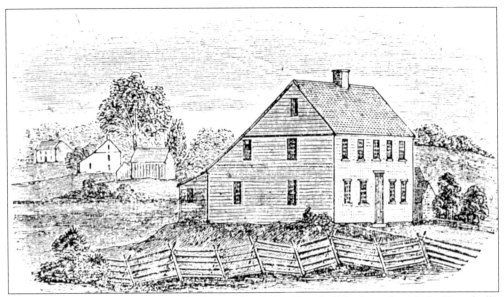

Another sketch by Barber shows the house that John Trumbull built in the 1740s. Trumbull's son, who was also named John, was born in this house in 1750. A brilliant lad, he entered Yale at 13 and was admitted to the bar in 1773. He was an important poet of the Revolution, and his satire M'*Fingal* did much to arouse the spirit of patriotism and strengthen the determination of the young republic to carry the issue to a successful conclusion.

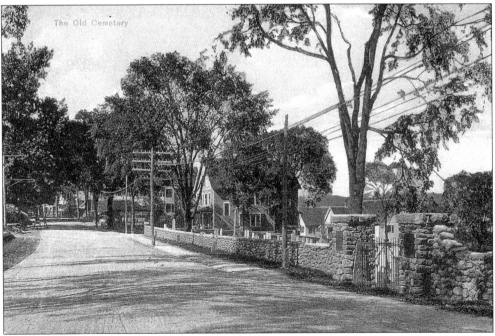

This is the wall that surrounds the old cemetery on Main Street. This area was set aside in 1740 to be used as a burial ground. The first burial was Hannah Richards (wife of Lt. William Scovill), who died on April 1, 1741, at the age of 39. The grounds were used until 1854, when Evergreen Cemetery was established. The stones for the wall were obtained from the Matoon farm.

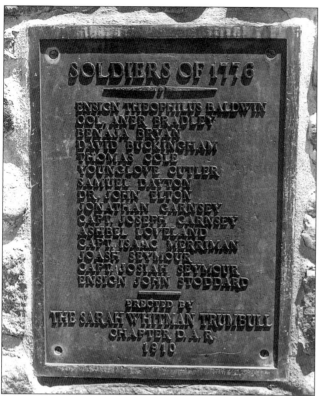

In 1910, plaques listing some of the 48 Revolutionary War soldiers from Watertown who are buried in the old cemetery were placed on each side of the gate by the Daughters of the American Revolution (DAR). In 1989, the DAR placed a plaque on a boulder by the back gate of the cemetery dedicated to Sarah Hosking for her service while a member of the organization.

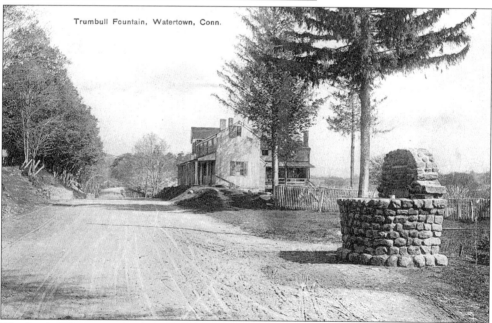

The Sarah Whitman Trumbull Chapter of the DAR erected this fountain in 1905 to mark the site of Rev. John Trumbull's first house in Watertown. It was located 140 feet northeast of this spot. The fountain is gone, but the plaque hangs between two posts. The building in the background, opposite Trumbull Street, was Joseph Hickox's tin shop.

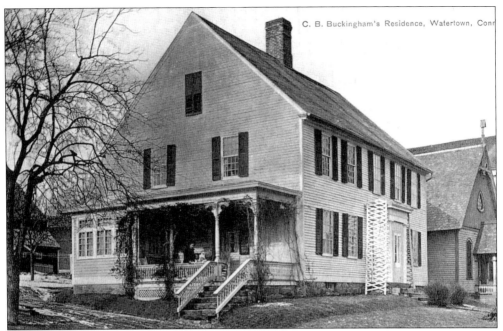

This house was built in 1772 by Rev. John Trumbull. Col. Edmund Lockwood added a large ballroom in 1794, and it became a well-known tavern. David Woodward ran the tavern from 1812 to c. 1850 and then used it as a residence. In 1905, Charles and Agnes Buckingham purchased the house, and in 1957 it again became the Congregational parsonage.

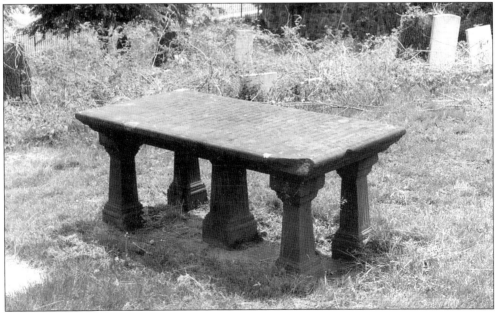

This tabletop stone marks the final resting place for Rev. John Trumbull. He died on December 13, 1787, at age 73, after serving as minister of the Congregational church for 48 years. After the second church was erected in 1772, Trumbull built the house next to the present-day church. The members of the Daughters of the American Revolution are responsible for the upkeep of the cemetery.

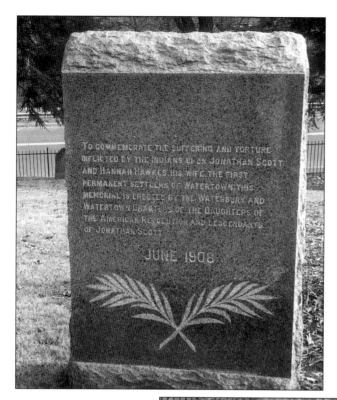

This monument to Jonathan and Hannah Hawks Scott was dedicated on June 3, 1908, to commemorate the suffering inflicted on them by Native Americans. In the early 1700s, several members of their family were killed by Native Americans. Jonathan and his two sons were captured and taken to Canada. He returned with one of his sons and built the first sawmill in the Greenville section of Westbury.

Michael Dayton was born in New Haven, Connecticut, in 1722. He and his wife, Mehitable, moved to Watertown c. 1750. The family owned a large tract of land here and had 13 children. Dayton served in the Revolutionary War and died on September 22, 1776, four months after being discharged. On November 15, 1985, the new bridge on French Street was dedicated to the Dayton family.

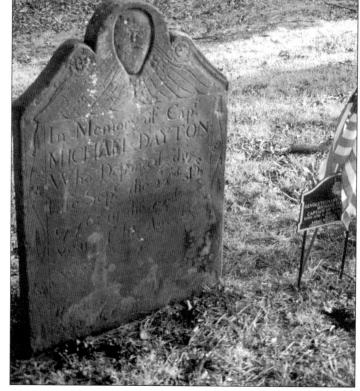

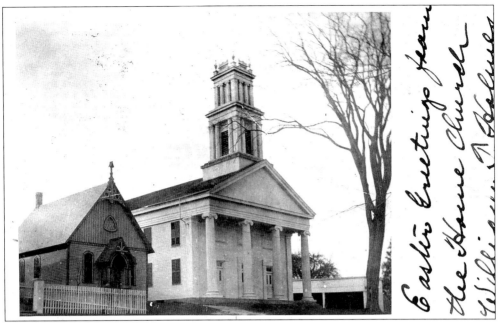

The third Congregational church, pictured here, was placed in the Connecticut Register of Historic Places on August 19, 1966. The small building on the left is a chapel that was built in 1870. It was demolished when an addition was made to the church in 1914. To the right of the church are the horse sheds where the animals were protected from the weather while people worshiped.

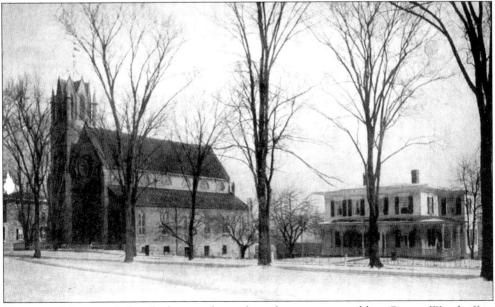

The second Episcopal church that was located on the green was sold to George Woodruff in 1854 for $300 and moved to Woodruff Avenue, where it became Citizens Hall. The church in this photograph was built in 1855 and used until 1923, when it was taken down and the present-day stone structure was built. The building on the right is the rectory before the third floor was added.

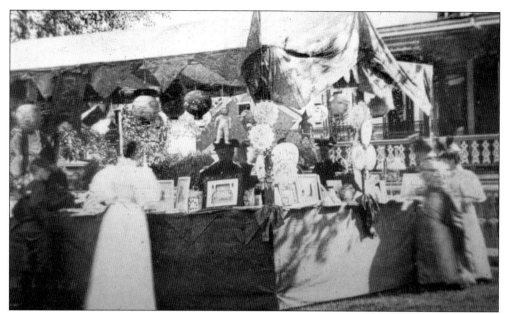

In the 1890s, the ladies of the Episcopal church held an annual outdoor event called Al Fresco Fete on the green that is owned by the church. Booths were set up, and there were lemonade stands, ice-cream stands, and an outdoor restaurant. A phonograph provided music during the day, but at night, live bands played for dancing. One year, a gypsy camp was a great attraction.

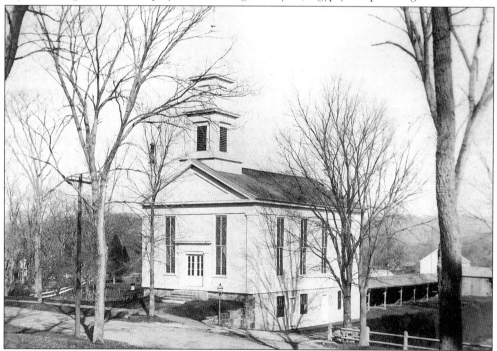

The first Methodist church was built on Strait's Turnpike near the Morris town line in 1838. Desiring a place closer to town, the members met in the ballroom of Gen. Merrit Heminway's hotel in the summer of 1853, and they rented the Congregational Chapel for winter services. The church shown here, complete with horse sheds, was dedicated in 1854.

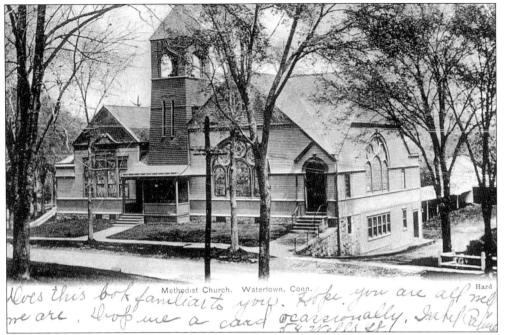

Methodist Church. Watertown, Conn.

Does this look familiar to you. Hope you are all well we are. Drop me a card occasionally. Jack (Raffe) 54 Wells St. Hard

Augustus Woolson purchased the old Methodist church for $1,000 and raised $9,500 for a new church. This larger building with a belfry was built in 1897. The horse sheds remained until the automobile replaced the horse.

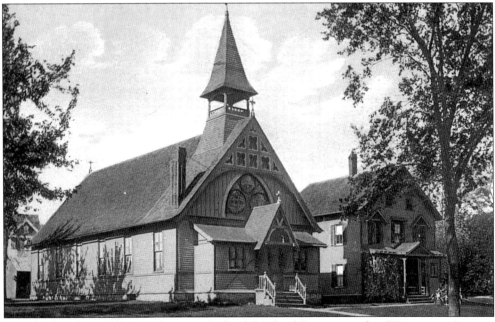

Shortly after the great potato famine in Ireland, Michael Dunn arrived in Watertown. As more Catholic families migrated, they gathered at homes to conduct worship services. As the number increased, services were held in Citizens Hall. Finally, this church was built on the corner of Main Street and Woodruff Avenue and was dedicated on March 24, 1878. The building on the right was the rectory. A school was built in 1907.

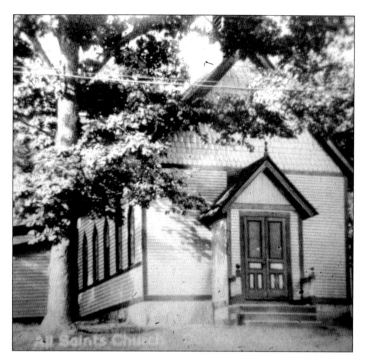

The people of the Episcopal faith who lived in Oakville held services as early as 1850 in the "webb shop," presumably the old suspender shop just over the line in Waterbury. By 1887, they had moved to Temperance Hall. All Saint's Church was built between 1903 and 1906. When a larger building was needed, they erected a new structure that was dedicated in 1960.

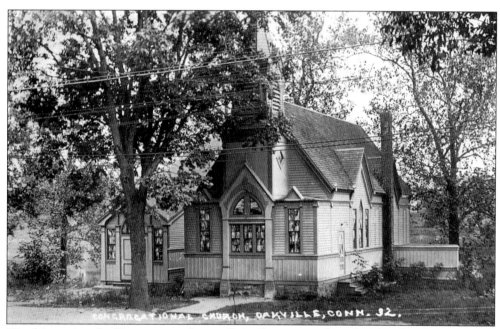

Worship services for Congregationalists in Oakville were conducted in the old school on Main Street, first by the YMCA of Waterbury and then by the minister of the second Congregational church. In 1877, the Waterbury church gave $1,200 to build this Oakville Chapel on the west side of Main Street. A new church on Buckingham Street was completed in 1961.

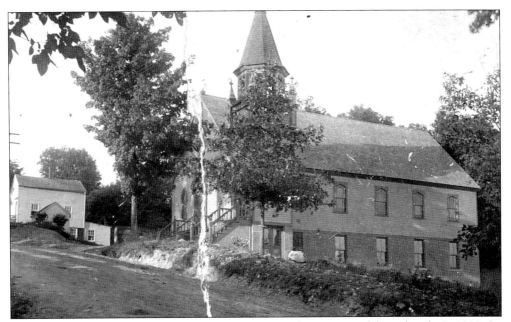

As the Catholic population in the Oakville area grew, there was need for a church. In 1900, St. Mary Magdalen Church was erected on Buckingham Street. By 1952, there was a need for a larger structure. While the new church was being built on the corner of Buckingham and Main Streets, the old wooden structure burned. Later, a school was erected at the intersection of Buckingham Street and Hillside Avenue.

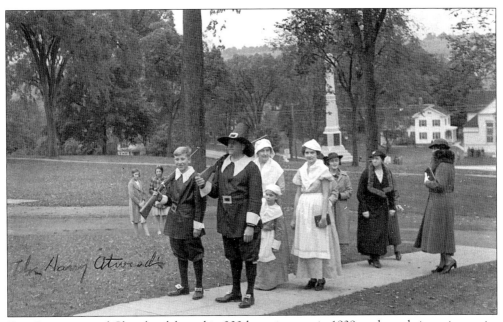

First Congregational Church celebrated its 200th anniversary in 1939, and people in puritan attire attended the service. This is the Harry Atwood family as they walked up to the church. Harry Atwood had a used-car lot on the corner of Main and Belden Streets for many years. His son Donald, who is on the left in the picture, was owner of Baronian Insurance at the same location.

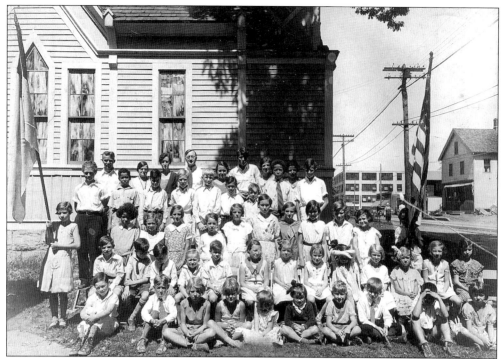

The members of the Union Congregational Church Sunday school are shown outside the church on Main Street when Rev. Oscar Locke was the pastor, c. the 1930s. He is pictured wearing glasses in the back row.

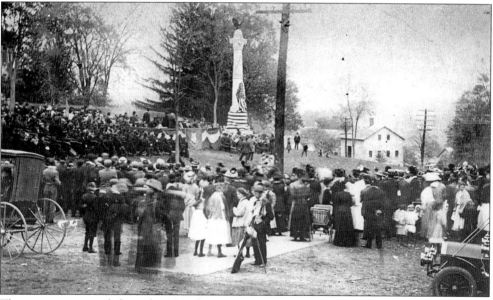

This monument was dedicated on October 10, 1908, to the 130 men from Watertown who served in the Civil War. The memorial is 36 feet high and has a 12-foot base. There is a bronze eagle on the top, and around the shaft are carved the names of the battles in which Watertown men took part. Bronze tablets bear the names of the men who served their country in the Civil War.

Pictured is 1st Lt. William W. Lewis of Watertown. He served in Company D during the Civil War until his promotion to captain of Company B on November 20, 1863. He was wounded at Winchester on September 19, 1864.

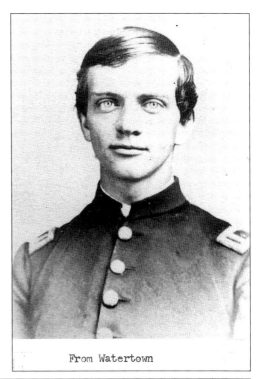

From Watertown

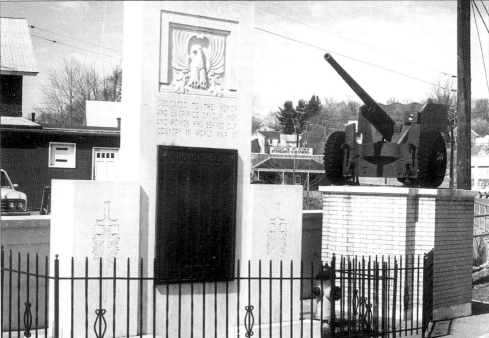

Soon after the end of World War II, the people of Oakville collected money to build this monument, complete with cannon, by the bridge across Steele Brook. After the demolition of the factory on the corner of Main and Riverside Streets, a beautiful park was developed and the monument and cannon found a new home.

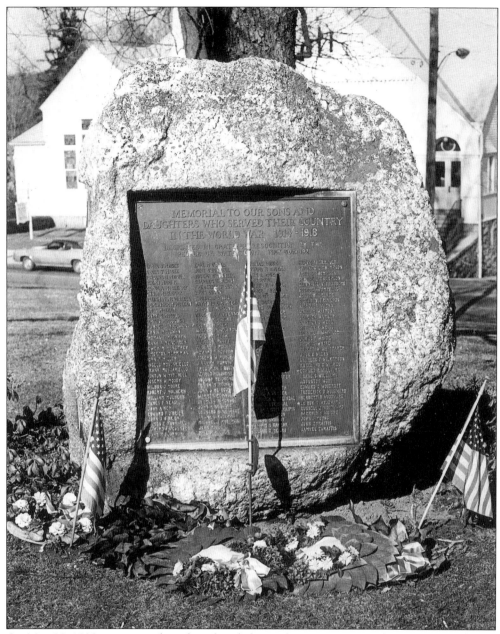

On May 30, 1920, many people gathered to dedicate this monument to the approximately 200 young men and a few nurses from Watertown who saw action in World War I. About a dozen of these men were killed and are buried in Europe. The boulder, estimated to weigh 12 tons, was found in Woodbury. Nine sturdy horses were used to move this stone, and it was placed on a heavy-duty wagon (which weighed about 10 tons) and moved to this site. Wreaths are placed at this monument each Memorial Day and Veterans Day in memory of these heroic men and women.

Two

TRAINS, TROLLEYS, CARS, AND PLANES

Early traveling in Watertown was by horse and buggy. Stagecoaches, which stopped at three taverns in town, were the only means by which people could travel to distant locations, until the Watertown and Waterbury Railroad was incorporated on June 23, 1869. This shows the names of some of the subscribers for stock in the railroad. S. Whitter, agent for the town, purchased $65,000 worth of stock.

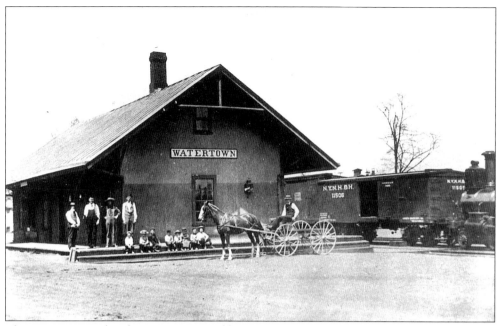

The Watertown railroad station is pictured here c. 1890. Railroad traffic continued to increase, and by 1900, there were 12 trains coming from Waterbury to Watertown daily. The president of the railroad was O.B. King, owner and operator of the Warren House, an active hotel from 1866 to 1890.

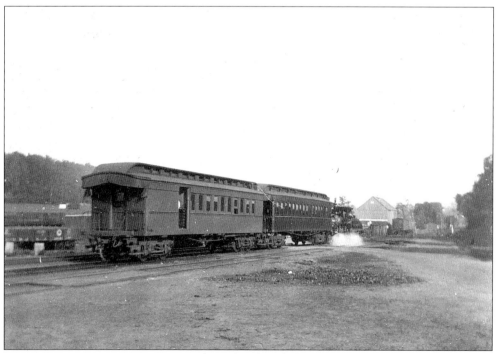

Passenger cars were a common site at the railroad yards for many years. This 1898 photograph shows two cars that were used by many residents who worked in Waterbury and other areas of Connecticut.

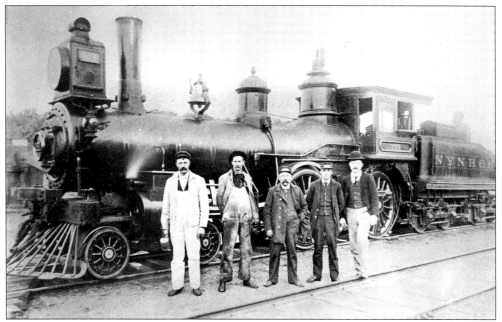

This is "Old Number 191," an engine that hauled the Watertown train for many years. This photograph was taken *c.* 1900 and includes, from left to right, Tom Fray, engineer; an unidentified fireman; Clarence Cook, conductor; Henry Fairclough, brakeman; and Eugene Wheeler, agent.

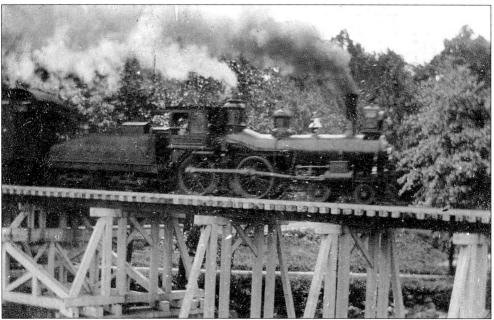

The railroad went bankrupt in 1875, and the state of Connecticut took it over. It became a part of the Naugatuck Railroad and was later leased to the New York, New Haven, and Hartford Railroad. Here is "Old Number 191" as it went across the bridge near the Seymour Smith and Sons Company on Main Street in Oakville. On the 4.9-mile track, there were bridges as well as ground-level crossings.

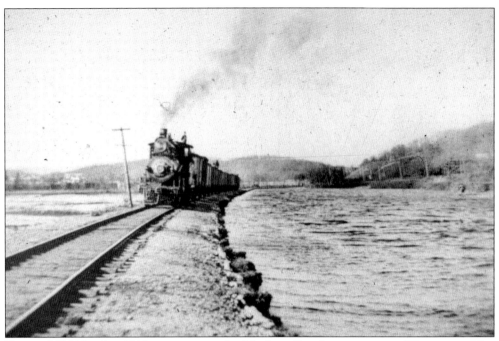

Here is "Old Number 191" coming past the Manhan Canal on its way to Watertown. This photograph was taken in 1897.

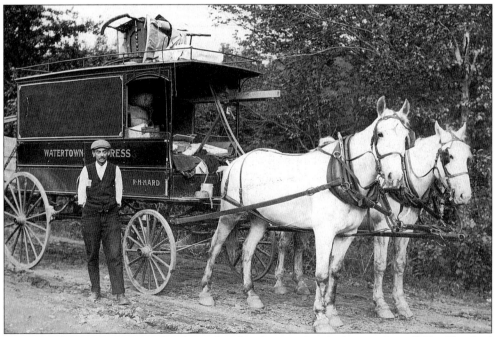

Many people in Watertown ordered merchandise from mail-order houses. Russell Hard hitched up his team, met the trains, loaded the goods on his "Watertown Express," and delivered the items to the proper location.

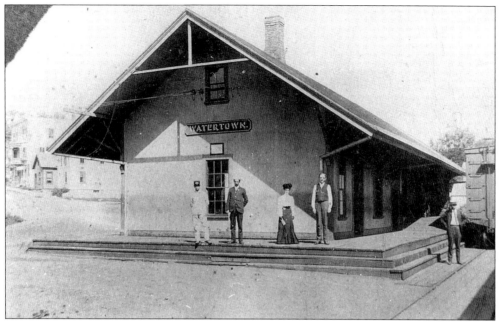

The station was described at the time of its opening as "a neat building 30' by 60'—ladies and gents rooms, ticket office, baggage and freight offices." Water was piped from a spring in the hill, and there was an engine house and a turntable. This is a view of the station in 1897.

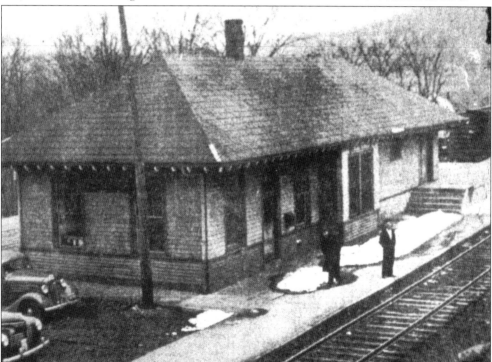

This is the Oakville railroad station that was located on Falls Avenue. The station burned to the ground in the 1950s. The cement steps leading to the platform can be seen today in what is now a wooded area.

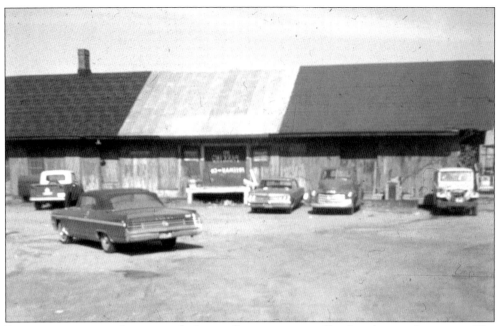

Passenger service was discontinued when trolley service was offered to the people in town. The Interstate Commerce Commission decided to abandon the railroad on January 23, 1973. The last train came into town in February 1974. This photograph shows the depot in 1965 before it was demolished and the Depot Mall was constructed on the site.

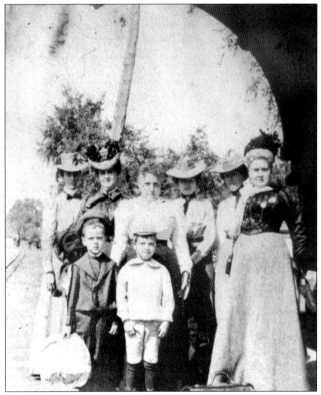

Many Smith families lived in the area of the Seymour Smith and Sons Company. The small building shown in this photograph was erected by the railroad track behind what is now Ro's Restaurant. It was called Welton's Station, and the train only stopped when flagged. Members of the Smith family are shown waiting for the train.

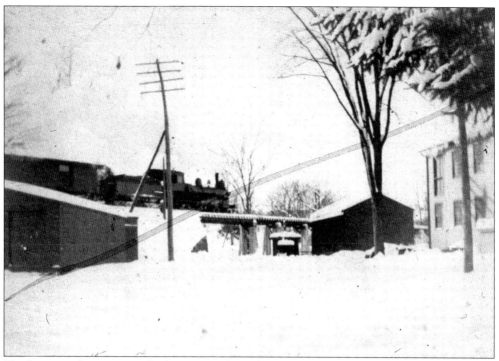

Tracks were always in need of repair, and much of the work was done on Sunday to avoid interfering with weekday traffic. This image shows the crew working on the trestle near the Seymour Smith factory.

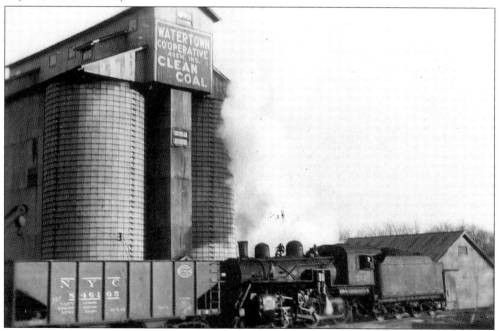

The Watertown Cooperative Association building was on Depot Street across from the railroad station. This view shows the storage tanks used for coal. Trains would bring the coal to Watertown, and it would be stored in the tanks and later delivered to their customers.

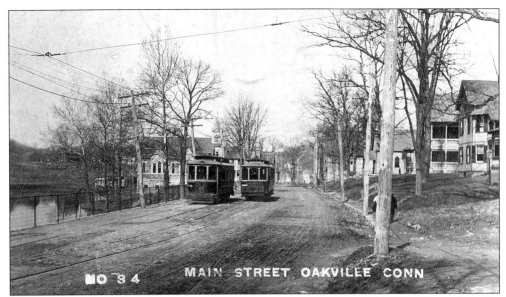

The railroad had been transporting people to and from Waterbury for almost 30 years when the Connecticut Railway and Lighting Company began laying trolley tracks along Main Street in Oakville *c*. 1894. Pin Shop Pond switch, shown in this photograph, was installed, making it possible to have two trolleys on the track at any time.

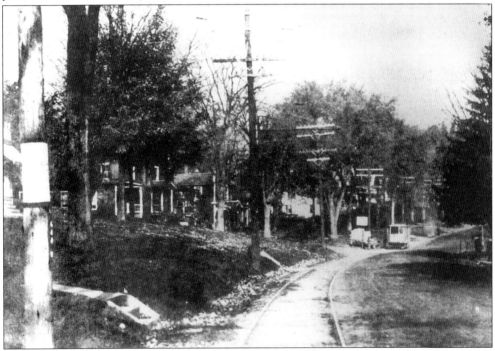

Tracks were eventually laid to Warren Way, with Woodruff switch, Ads switch, and Cemetery switch added along the way. Here is a trolley coming down Main Street near Echo Lake Road in 1908. For 30 years, people rode the trolley. For the last trip from Watertown on May 23, 1937, more than 80 people crowded into trolley car No. 3132. Everything was stripped from the car as souvenirs.

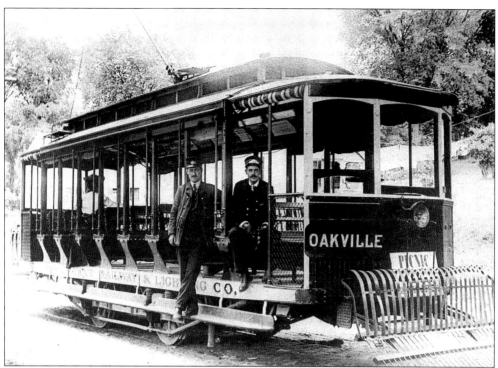

Each summer, the children in Union Congregational Church Sunday school took the trolley to Lake Quassapaug for a day's outing. The conductors here are waiting for the children to board.

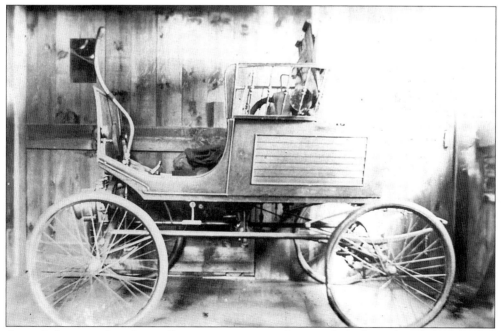

Around the time that the trolley came to town, a few people had purchased the horseless carriage. One of the first cars in Watertown was this one, which belonged to James B. Woolson.

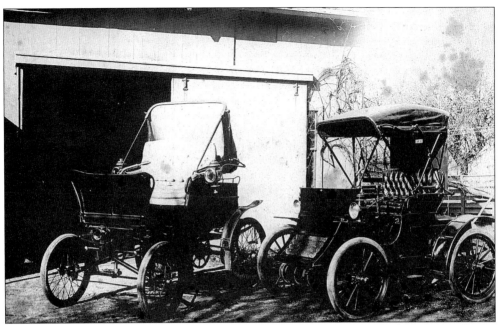

Dr. E.K. Loveland was a physician in Watertown for many years. He used a horse and buggy, but was later seen driving these early cars that are shown by his carriage house at 60 North Street. The Loveland family lived in the Greek revival house at 48 North Street for 75 years. Eli Curtiss built this house in 1837 and had his Marino sheep farm here.

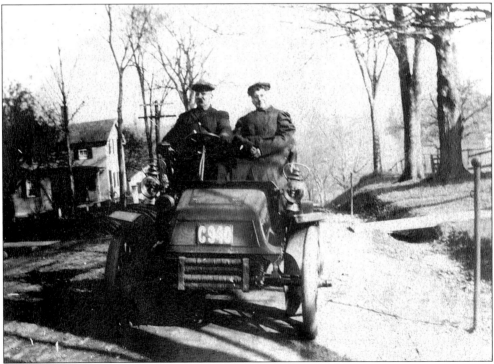

Another of the first cars in Watertown was the one that belonged to the Warners, who are shown driving up Cutler Street in the early 1900s.

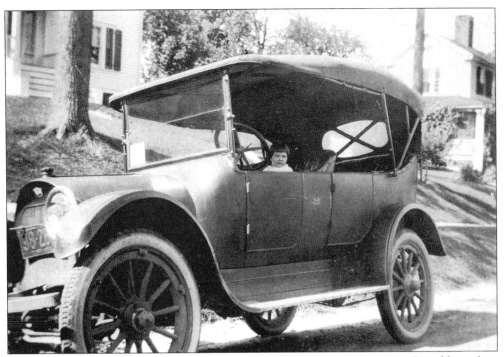

Touring cars like this were seen for many years on the streets in Watertown. In cold weather, side curtains would cover the windows.

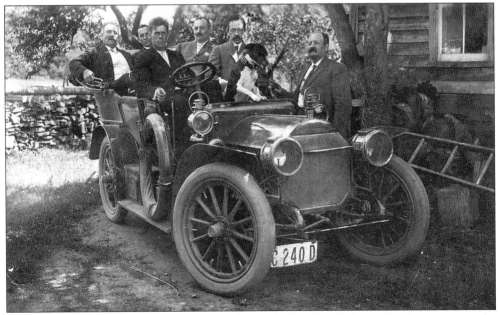

James Strockbine, shown standing on the right, worked at the Hitchcock hardware store in the Pythian building on Main Street. He was often seen taking his friends and his dog for a ride in this fancy automobile.

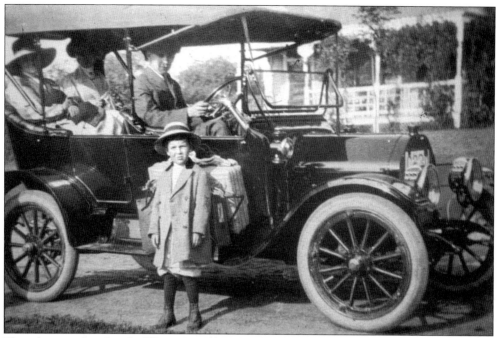

This photograph, taken by Watertown photographer Harry Hard, shows the Warner family of Oakville going for a Sunday drive. The picture was taken in front of the Baird house in Oakville.

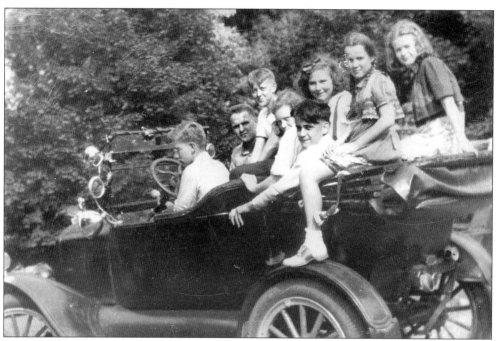

Don Atwood, whose father owned a used-car lot on lower Main Street, was one of the few high school students who had "wheels" in the 1930s. He is shown taking his friends for a ride. From left to right are Don Atwood, George McCleary, Willard Booth, Nancy Parker, Bob Hayward, Beth Olson, Jane McCleary, and Nancy McGee.

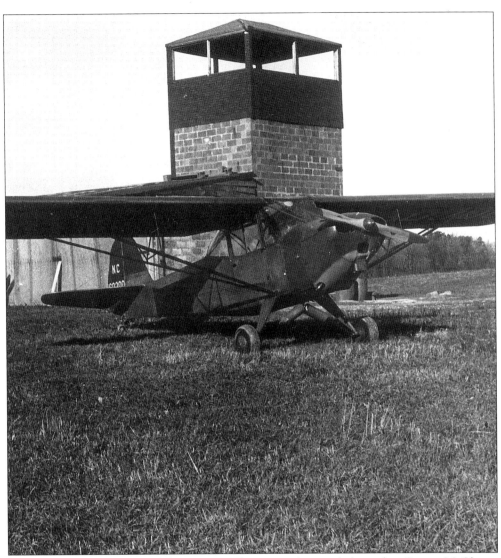

This plane, shown in front of the tower at Watertown Airport, belonged to George McCleary. The commercial operation, started at the airport in 1946, folded after a few years. Private pilots rented it from Bob Wookey until a terrible windstorm demolished the hanger and planes in June 1950. This land was later used for free-flight model airplanes. Some of the Watertown men who flew at this airport were George Barnes, George McCleary, John Hayward, Willard Booth, Ray Bellemare, Livingston Crowell, Henry Long, and Reinhold DeWitt. Houses on Lexington Drive, Concord Drive, and Mystic Lane were built on the location of the old airport on Bunker Hill Road.

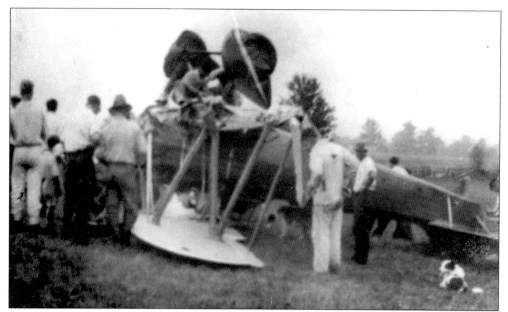

During an eclipse of the sun in 1936, the pilot of this army plane tried to land in a field off Guernseytown Road. The field was wet and the plane flipped over. It was dismantled and, when a crew attempted to remove it, their vehicle became stuck and needed to be pulled out by a team of horses. People picked up small pieces of wood from the wreckage as souvenirs.

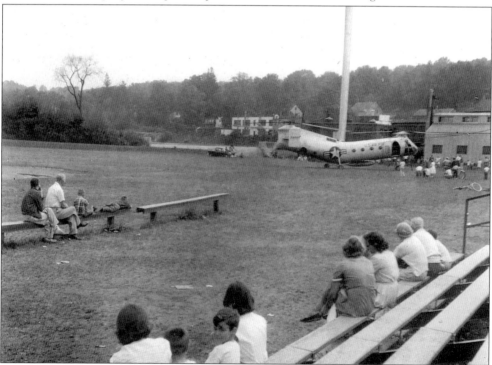

On a summer afternoon in 1959, this military helicopter developed a mechanical problem, circled over Watertown for a while, and eventually landed at Deland Field. Many residents got their first good look at a helicopter while the engine was being repaired.

Three
INNS, HOTELS, AND EARLY INDUSTRY

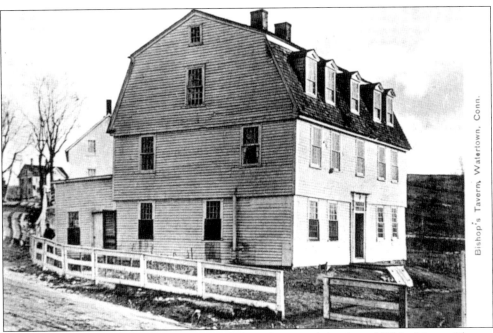

Bishop's Tavern, Watertown, Conn.

Noah Judd built this tavern on the corner of Main Street and Academy Hill for his son Eleazer, who ran the establishment for many years. This was one of the most famous taverns in the northwest corner of the state. James Bishop, a merchant and farmer, took over the tavern when room and board was $1.50 a week. Merrit Heminway boarded at the tavern so he could attend school in town. He was eventually hired to work in the store that Bishop ran in the basement of the tavern. By 1850, Heminway became the owner of the tavern and all of the land nearby. When Heminway started his silk factory, he moved this building to Echo Lake Road, and his employees lived there. It is now Daveluy's Restaurant.

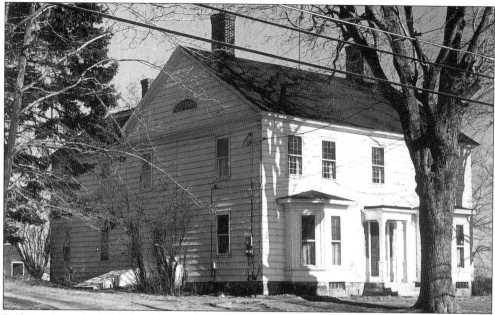

Built in the early 1830s by Sabra and Selah Scoville, this tavern provided a resting place for weary stage drivers and travelers. Watertown was at the crossroads of two stagecoach routes. On the route from New Haven to Litchfield, the Scoville Tavern was an important rest stop. This place was known for its oyster stew and for the dances held on the second floor.

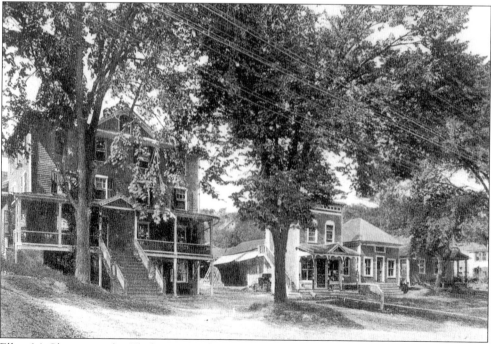

Ellen McCleary ran the Elmhurst Hotel on Main Street for many years in the early 1900s. Located opposite Depot Street, it was a convenient stop for train passengers until it burned down c. 1930. McCleary was a businesswoman and owned much property in town. She had a store on French Street and built a miniature golf course on Woodbury Road.

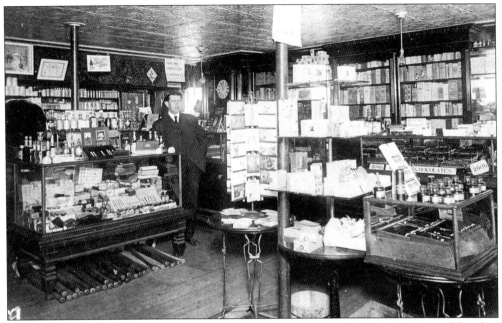

Daniel Sullivan graduated from college and came to Watertown, where he opened his first drugstore at the corner of Depot and Main Streets in 1899. This photograph shows Sullivan in his well-stocked store. Ten years later, he moved to the brick building at the corner of Main Street and Echo Lake Road, where he had an ice-cream parlor.

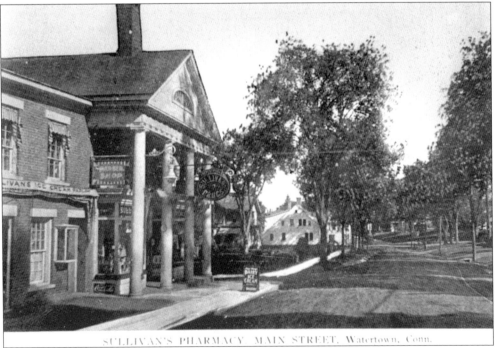

SULLIVAN'S PHARMACY, MAIN STREET, Watertown, Conn.

Gen. Merrit Heminway and James Bishop built this brick store, Bishop and Heminway, across the street from Bishop's Tavern. It was Sullivan's Drug Store for 10 years, a bank for many years, and is now a restaurant. The telephone company office was located in the rear of the building.

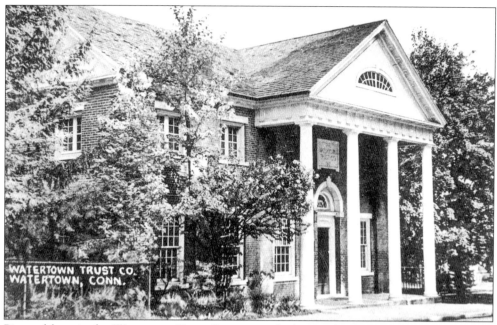

Pictured here is the Watertown Trust Company, which was the first bank in town. It later became the Colonial Bank and Trust Company. Gen. Merrit Heminway used the back of this building as a factory where he wound thread on spools.

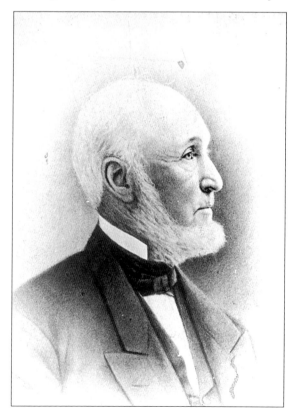

The Heminway and Sons Silk Company was incorporated in 1847, and the first factory was built on Echo Lake Road. Gen. Merrit Heminway was the first person in the world to wind silk thread on spools. Prior to this, it had been sold in skeins. Spooled silk became necessary when the sewing machine was invented.

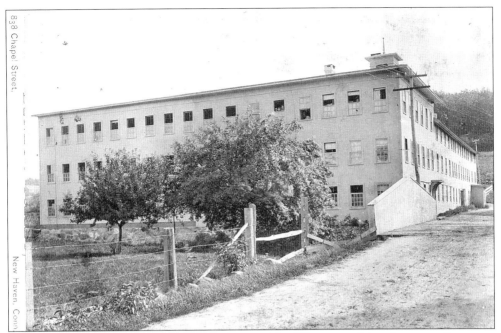

This was Heminway's Echo Lake Road factory. The Watertown Manufacturing Company, maker of composition buttons and molded electrical parts, took over this building in 1915. The company produced Melamine dishes used on navy ships in World War II. After the war, the company made Lifetime Ware for domestic use. This product was designed by Jon Hedu, for which he received many awards.

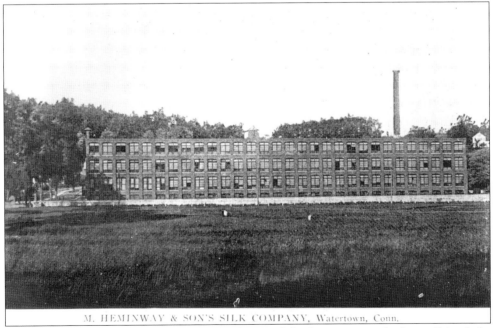

M. HEMINWAY & SON'S SILK COMPANY, Watertown, Conn.

This second building of the Heminway and Sons Silk Company was built on Echo Lake Road in 1916. It has housed the Princeton Knitting Mills, Timex, and is now a part of the Siemon Complex.

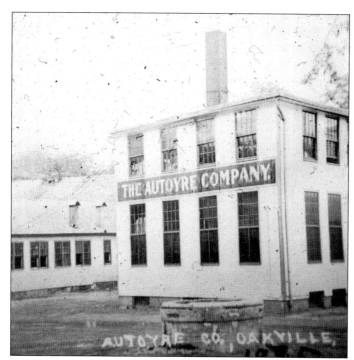

After the Warner house at the corner of Hillside Avenue and Riverside Street was moved from this location, Joseph Baird opened a small plant on the site. The Autoyre Company was incorporated in 1912 and made bathroom fixtures, fruit jar trimmings, bottle openers, and countless household items. Ekco Company bought out the Autoyre and, in a few years, moved out of town.

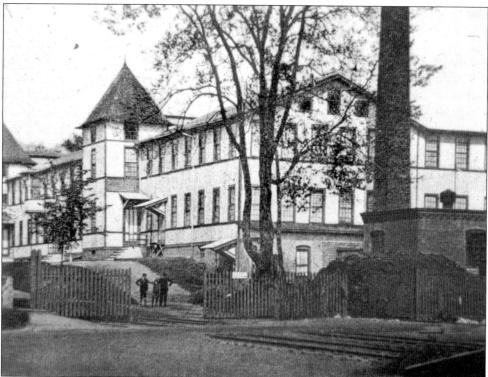

When Gen. Merrit Heminway died, his son Buel joined with William Bartlett and formed the Heminway and Bartlett Silk Company in this building on Echo Lake Road. The company later moved to the industrial park off Buckingham Street.

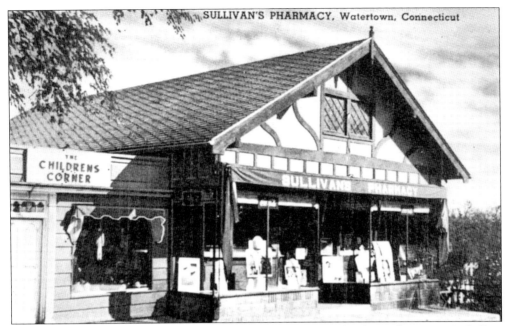

SULLIVAN'S PHARMACY, Watertown, Connecticut

This was Sullivan's Drug Store for almost 50 years. During the flu epidemic in 1918, Dan Sullivan and daughter Alice, who had graduated from the school of pharmacy, worked day and night compounding prescriptions while Mrs. Sullivan and son George delivered them. Baldwin School students would walk to the store during lunch hour to buy penny candy. The Children's Corner was located here as well.

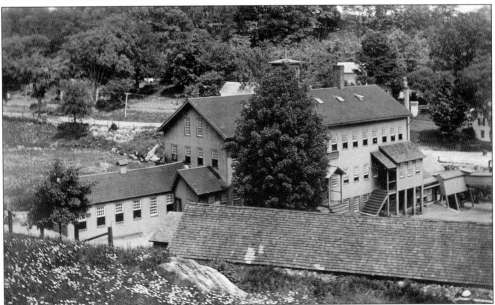

In 1720, Jonathan Scott built a gristmill on this site, where he ground corn for local farmers. A.B. Everett and Friend Davis opened a small shop here, where they made mousetraps. The factory burned in 1850 but was rebuilt and had 15 prominent Watertown stockholders. The Watertown Manufacturing Company proceeded to manufacture mousetraps, umbrella frames, sewing silk, and other goods.

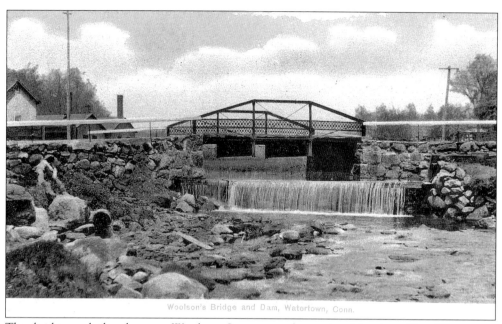

Woolson's Bridge and Dam, Watertown, Conn.

The bridge and the dam on Woolson Street are shown in this view. The Watertown Manufacturing Company buildings can be seen in the background. Many of the buildings were painted green, so this became known as the Greenville section of town. The factory eventually became the Woolson Manufacturing Company before closing in the mid-1920s. On April 28, 1930, someone doused it with gas and lit a match, destroying the factory.

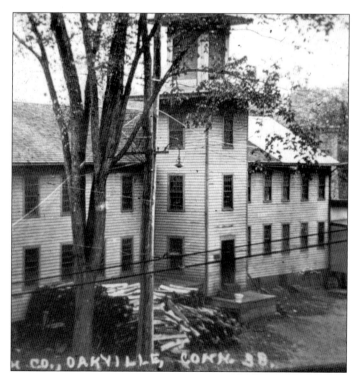

After Elias Howe patented the first sewing machine in 1846, Nathaniel Wheeler of Watertown made a greatly improved model in 1850 and formed the Wheeler Wilson Sewing Machine Company. This factory was located across from Ro's Restaurant. When a search for land proved fruitless, the company moved to Bridgeport and joined with the Singer Sewing Machine Company.

Wheeler Wilson sewing machines were sold all over the world. This is one of the machines that was made in Watertown, and it can be seen at the historical society museum.

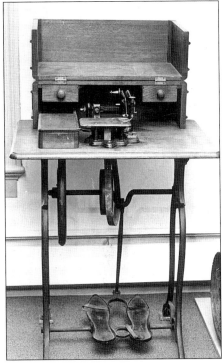

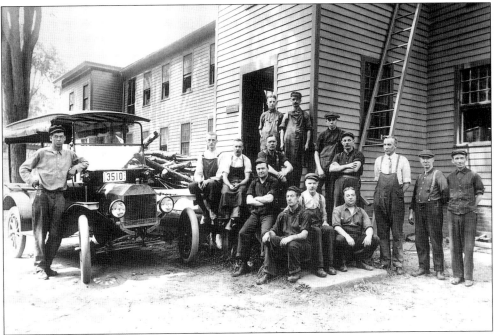

The Seymour Smith and Sons Company began its business in Worchester, Massachusetts, in 1850. The company moved to Sharon, Connecticut, and eventually to Oakville, where it purchased the Wheeler Wilson factory. Seymour Smith and Sons manufactured pruning shears, bullrings, and other metal products. A brick building replaced this one in 1928. These are employees of the company in 1916.

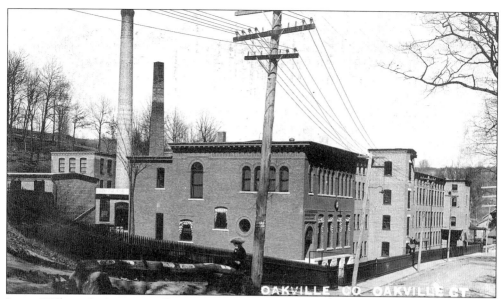

James Williams built a gristmill on this site, near the Waterbury town line, in 1729. The mill became the Oakville Pin Company, and the business became very successful. It later became a division of Scovill Manufacturing Company and employed thousands of people. It was vacant for years, but Maurice Fabiani has divided the building and most of it is being used by small companies.

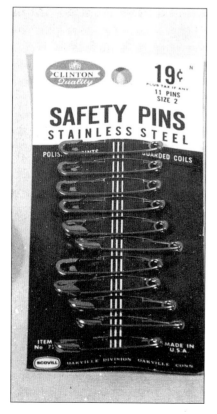

Because there was no automatic device for attaching safety pins to cards, many women went to the Oakville Pin Company and took them home to assemble by hand. Entire families would sit around the table and attach the pins for distribution.

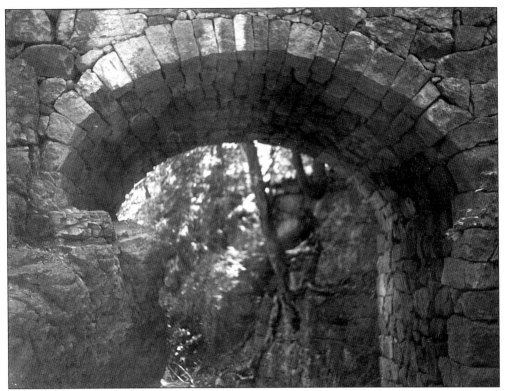

This keystone arch bridge—held together by a central stone at the top—was built *c.* 1866 on Skilton Road. During a storm in May 1984, the bridge developed a hole in the deck. It was rebuilt and, on December 10, 1991, became the first site in Watertown to be listed on the National Register of Historic Places.

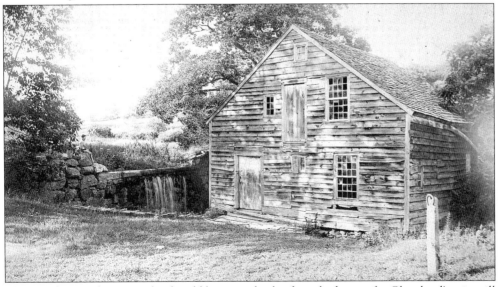

The first dam up the stream by the old keystone bridge furnished water for Cleveland's gristmill shown above. The dam is still there, but the mill has been gone for more than 80 years. In the 1920s, there was a clicking sound coming from the mechanism in the ground at that location.

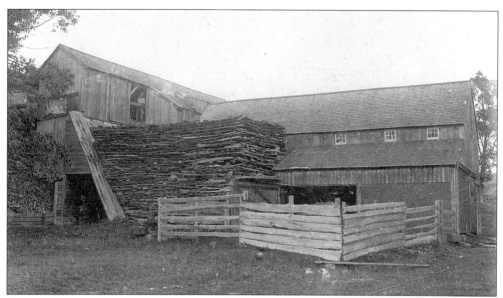

The second dam up the stream from the old keystone bridge furnished waterpower to Merritt Skilton's sawmill. As shown in the photograph, much lumber was cut at this mill. There were many apple orchards in Watertown, and in the lower left is a door to the area where Skilton made cider.

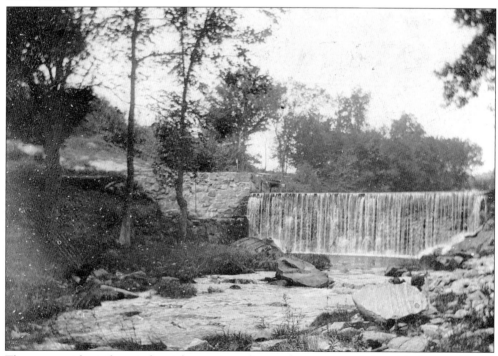

There were at least three industrial operations that used waterpower below this dam on Cherry Avenue. Bishop and Bradley made clocks, while knobs, faucets, toy carriages, and sleighs were manufactured in the Wheeler Shop. Homer Barlow acquired the Wheeler Shop by 1900, and he made items from sheep's wool. His principal items were a wall duster, a furniture duster, and a baby carriage robe.

Four

SCHOOLS, PUBLIC
AND PRIVATE

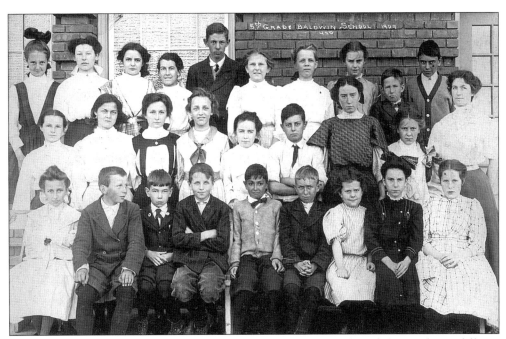

The Baldwin School second graders, shown here in 1909, are, from left to right, as follows: (front row) Hazel Bean, Dick Sperry, Stuart Atwood, Spencer Barlow, Sam Willinger, Joe Humiston, Justine McGowan, Vera McCleary, and Octavia Hickcox; (middle row) Nancy Bronson, Kate Herring, Naomi Davis, Laura Decker, Marilla Atwood, Harry Lockwood, Maude Vercher, and Marjorie Black; (back row) Barbara Bronson, Bertha Cook, Hattie Fields, Helen Matoon, Robert McCleary, Novello Fisher, Zelda Wheeler, Alice Norton, Fred White, and Charles Brouette. The teacher, a Miss Hurlbert, is on the right.

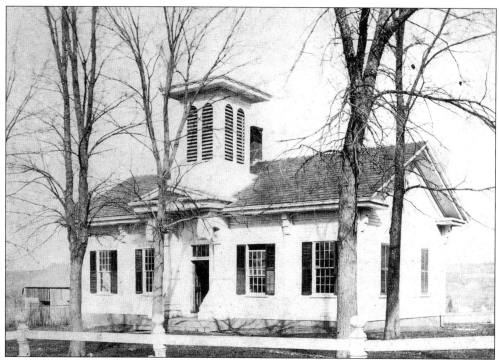

In 1852, Center School, built near the road on North Street, replaced the small school on the triangle. There were two rooms. Huge iron stoves provided heat for this school, and records tell us that in winter the children sitting near the stove "nearly baked" while those on the perimeter of the room "almost froze." This school was used until 1883.

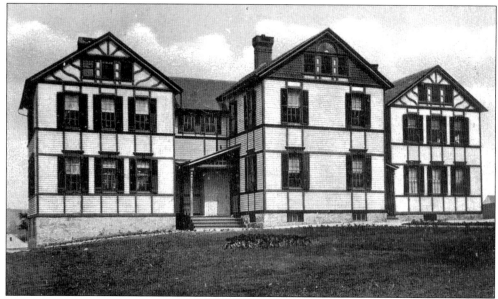

Because of the increase in population, a new four-room Center School was built just behind the first one in 1883, and an addition was made in 1894. At that time, there were 12 teachers employed in town at an average salary of $30.34 per month. On December 17, 1906, this building burned. Baldwin School, named for one of the early teachers, was erected on this site.

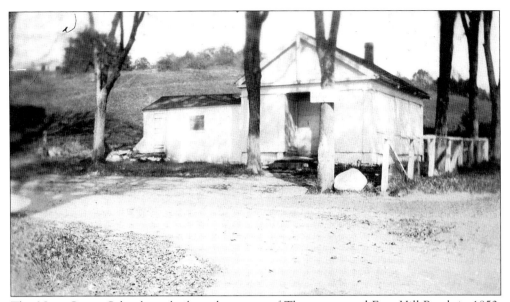

This Nova Scotia School was built at the corner of Thomaston and Fern Hill Roads in 1852. Classes ceased in 1929, and children were transported to Baldwin School. The school was given to the town. It was taken apart in September 1990 by members of UNICO Club, and in 1993, the Lions Club Old Fellows rebuilt it on Munson Park. The school is now open to the public.

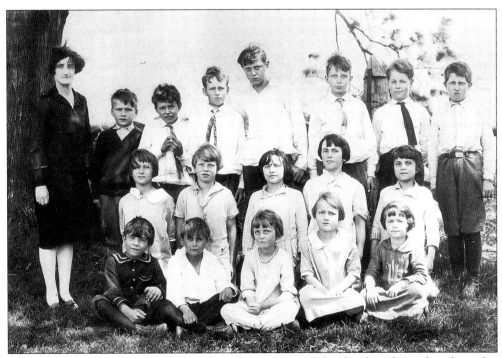

In the late 1920s, the students and teacher of Nova Scotia School gathered outside to have this picture taken. At this time, there was no running water in the school and no indoor plumbing. Boys and girls outhouses were provided, and the school was heated with a wood stove.

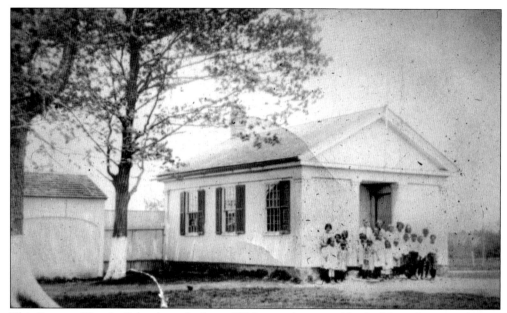

This Poverty District School was built in 1854 to replace an older building that was about a quarter mile west of here. In 1872, there were 13 students in the school. The name was changed to Winnemaug in 1910, and in 1932, classes ended here and children were transported to Baldwin School. The building was sold to the Winnemaug Social Club in 1935 and was destroyed by vandals in the 1950s.

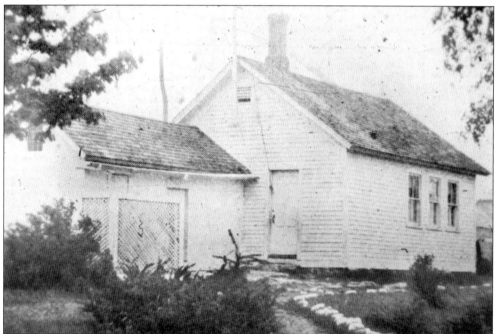

In 1848, this Guernseytown School was built to replace one that had burned. By the late 1920s, only students in grades one through three attended school here. Classes ended in 1931, and the children were transported to Baldwin School. In 1943, the building was sold for $100. It has been a residence since that time and has had several additions.

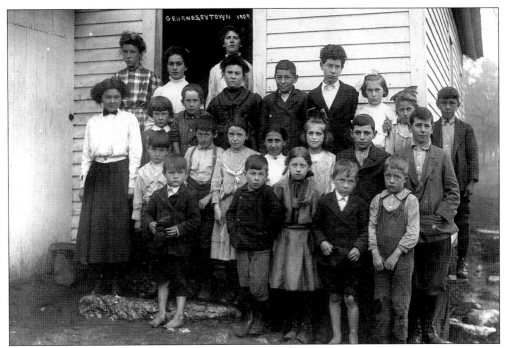

Pictured here is a Guernseytown School class in 1907. From left to right are the following: (front row) unidentified, Mike Sabot, Ted Blanner, Mary Wheeler, John Sabot, and Loren Wheeler; (middle row) Ella Little, Frank Judd, Freddie White, Harvey Williams, Dorothy Atwood, Annie Blanner, Maude Verba, Harry Weiss, and Garnsey Verba; (back row) Gladys Atwood, Julia Blanner, Annie Moriarity, Charlie Williams, Charlie Judd, Lillian Judd, Susie Williams, and Logie Blanner. Alice Sperry, the teacher, is standing in the door.

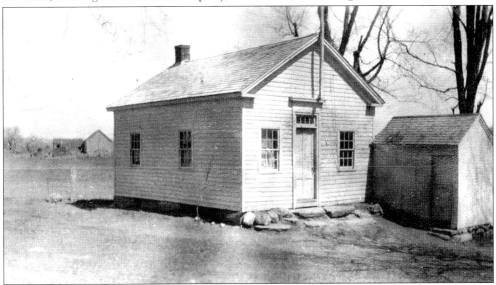

In 1854, this school was built to replace the former school in the French Mountain District of town, near the Morris town line. School visitor Horace Taft said in 1898, "Sanitary arrangement poor, school furniture antiquated and inconvenient." Classes ended here in 1929, and the children were transported to Baldwin School. The building was sold for $41.

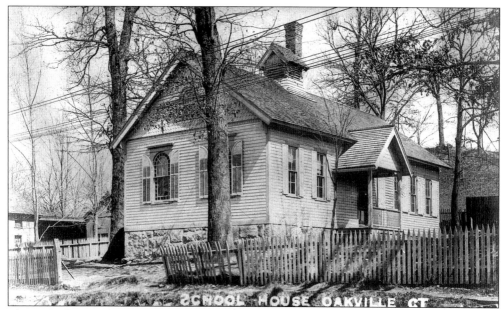

This Oakville District School was built in 1818 to replace an older one located on an adjoining lot. The name was changed to South School District in 1889. The building was moved back and a 20-foot addition was placed on the front. This building was sold when South School was built in 1909. It now belongs to All Saint's Church and is used for the Owl and the Pussy Cat Nursery School.

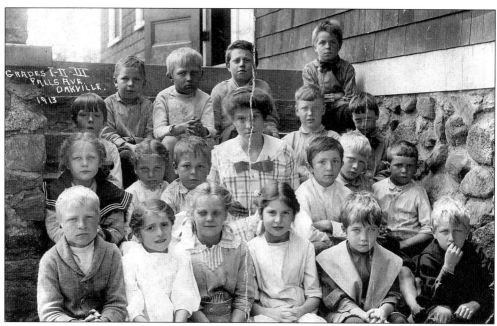

Grades one through three of Falls Avenue School are pictured in 1913. From left to right are the following: (front row) Charles Paul, Madeline Barberet, Theodote Mosgrove, unidentified, and Louis Prendely; (middle row) Rita Mosgrove, Mary Meissel, Pearly Bradshaw, ? Frost, Jules Barberet, Arthur Swanson, and Weldon Wheeler; (back row) Howard Bradshaw, Vincent Paul, Fred Emmons, Harry Ericson, Chester Smith, Harold Ryder, and Thomas Rutherford.

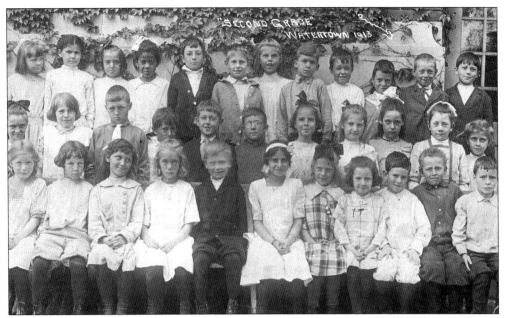

These second-grade students at Baldwin School are, from left to right, as follows: (front row) Ethelyn Harper, Carlton Seymour, Bertha Garber, Lois Doolittle, Peter Lund, Pearl Royce, Gertrude Stevens, Lucy Demarest, Thomas Maxwell, Arthur Litle, and Irving Dunston; (middle row) Helen Gater, Alice McCleary, Butler Bronson, unidentified, Frederick Hannon, Dudley Atwood, Ruth Patter, and Marion Barlow; (back row) three unidentified, ? Fitch, Myron Beale, Milton Dingwell, Earl Evans, Paul Johnson, two unidentified, and Raymond Davis.

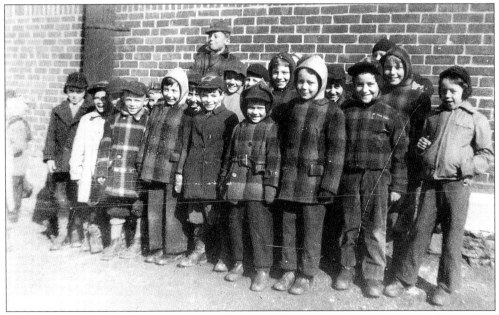

This picture of the first-grade students in Florence Thornhill's class at Polk School was taken on a cold day in February 1944. The students attended Polk School for kindergarten through third grade and then moved on to South School. Other teachers at the school at that time were Florence Gibbons, Constance Gibbons, and Eleanor Cook.

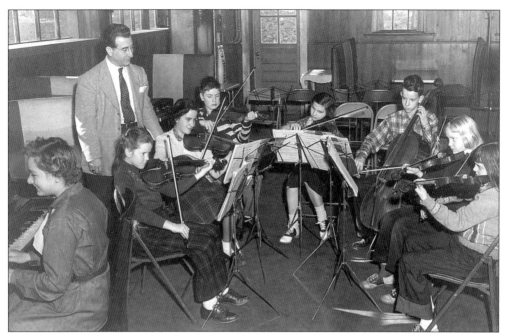

In the 1950s, Baldwin School became overcrowded and the junior orchestra practiced at the Youth Center, behind the Munson House. Sally Totten is playing the piano, and Penny Stearns is the blonde girl on the right. The Youth Center was open Friday nights, and Bernard Beauchamp was the director.

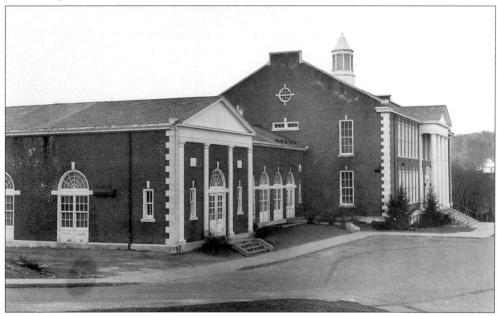

The first high school classes were held in the Academy. As additions were made to Center School, the upper floor was used for high school classes. These classes continued on the second floor when Baldwin School was built. In 1929, this new high school was erected and it was used until 1963, when the new school was built on French Street. The sixth-grade students now attend school here.

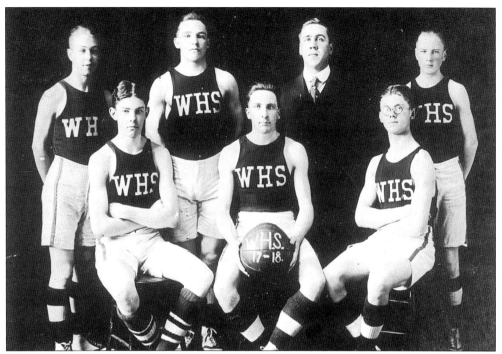

Watertown High School has had a basketball team for many years. This team played in the 1917–1918 season.

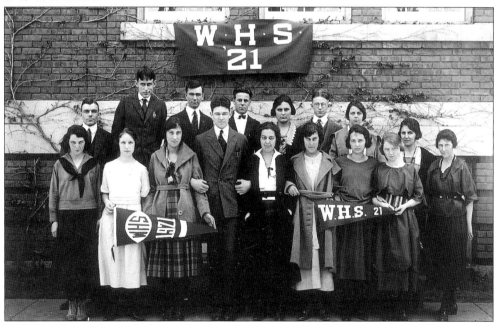

In 1921, Watertown High School was on the second floor of Baldwin School. The graduates that year were Grace O'Conner, Isabel Pope, Esther Hawser, George Sullivan, Hazel Quick, Sarah Johnson, Ruth Hauser, Catherine Castonbader, Marcel Roy, Starrs Hammond Knowlton, Francis Keilty, Art Jacobs, Leota Wigglesworth, Ed Hickcox, Erma Scott, and Ruth Strong. The teacher was Florence Bull.

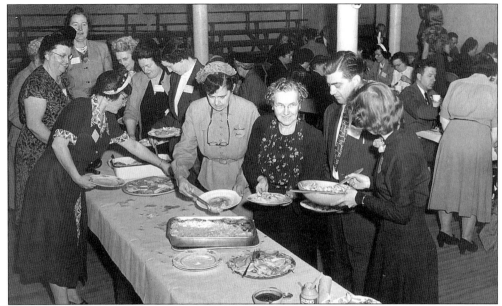

A School-Community-Industry Day was held in 1952, and townspeople were invited to go to the factories and the schools. This photograph shows people being served a ham dinner at South School. The woman third from the right is Frances Griffin. She taught at South School and then served as its principal for 25 years. The school was later named the Frances Griffin School.

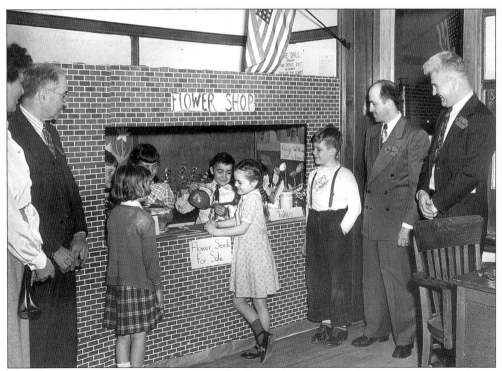

Some of the children at South School had a flower shop for the School-Community-Industry Day in 1952. Representatives of organizations and industries visited the shop that day.

Horace Taft ran a private boarding school for boys in Pelham, New York, in the early 1890s. Looking for a country setting for his school, he came to Watertown in 1893 and purchased a farmhouse on Buckingham Street. When he found that the Warren House was available, he gave up on his plan to build the school near his home. The residents of Watertown are fortunate to have such a great institution.

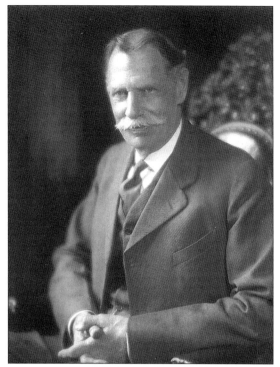

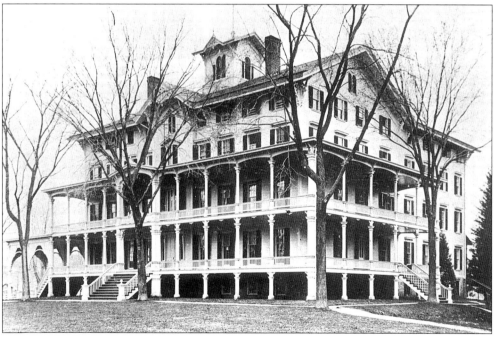

The owners of the Wheeler Wilson Sewing Machine Company built this grand Victorian hotel, the Warren House, in 1866. For some time, it was a summer vacation spot for city people. It was the town's showplace until it closed in 1890. When Horace Taft came to Watertown, he chose this as the location for his school. The building was demolished in 1929 and replaced by the Charles Phelps Taft Hall.

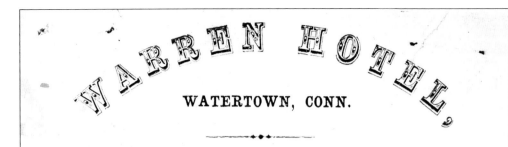

This advertisement from a New York paper in the 1860s enticed people from the city to vacation here. It was really a showplace and flourished after the railroad was built. At the close of the Watertown Fair each September, a huge ball was held at the Warren House.

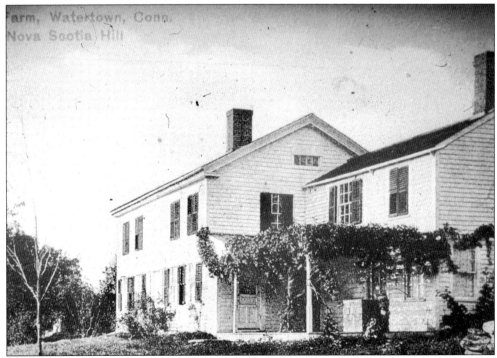

This is the house on Buckingham Street that Horace Taft purchased when he moved to Watertown. Today, there is evidence that a section of the basement of this house was used by the Underground Railroad. After Taft sold this house, other residents were Dr. Wilber Caney and family, as well as the William Ryder family.

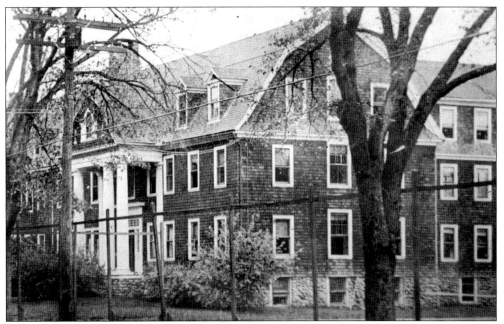

As space at the Warren House became a problem, Taft built the annex across the street from the school on the corner of Woodbury and Middlebury Roads. This building housed faculty and students and served the school well until brick dorms were erected. It was then demolished and the area is now used for parking.

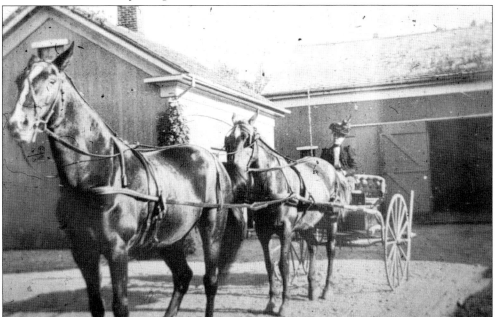

When Pres. William Howard Taft came to town to attend the funeral of his sister-in-law Winnie Taft (wife of Horace), Annie Buckingham (wife of John) sent her closed carriage to the railroad station to transport him to the school. Because of his size, the president became stuck in the door and was given a push by his aide. Annie Buckingham sent an open carriage for the return trip.

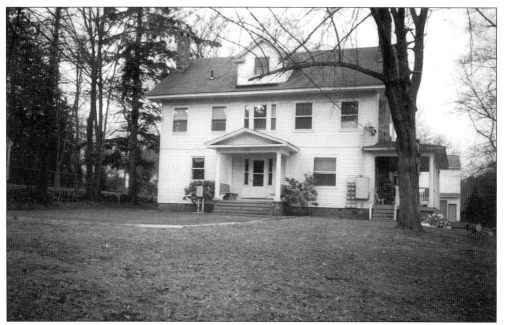

For many years, Fred and Alice Bassett owned this farmhouse at 306 Woodbury Road. It was the Country Day School from 1936 until it closed in 1941, and the house was made into apartments. Many servicemen returning from military duty after World War II found these small two- and three-room apartments a stopgap until they could purchase a home of their own.

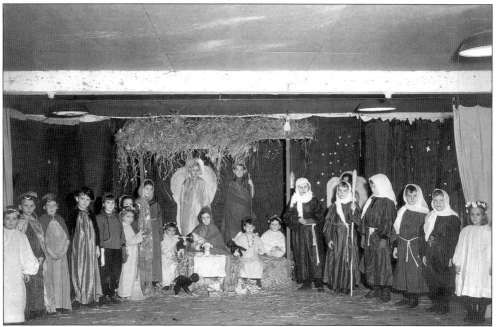

The Country Day School was a progressive institution where children were encouraged to follow their interests. The students at the school presented many performances in the barn, such as this 1937 Christmas play. Some of the children shown are Joe Spalding, John Chase, Karen Morgan, Sidney Wabber, Tony Chase, Lang Heminway, and Tom Quea Jr.

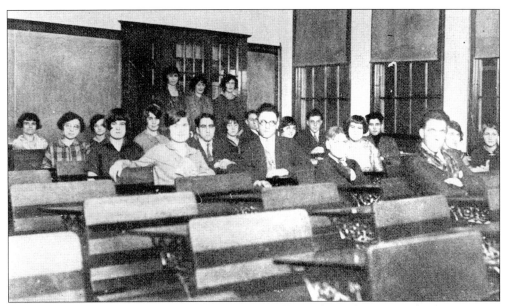

Many immigrants settled in Watertown and Oakville in the early 1990s. The Civic Union sponsored an Americanization class, which was later taught under the auspices of the Adult Education Association. Not only did Frances Griffin teach at South School, but she also taught this class for many years. This photograph shows one of the classes in 1927. Note the old school double desks that are attached to the floor.

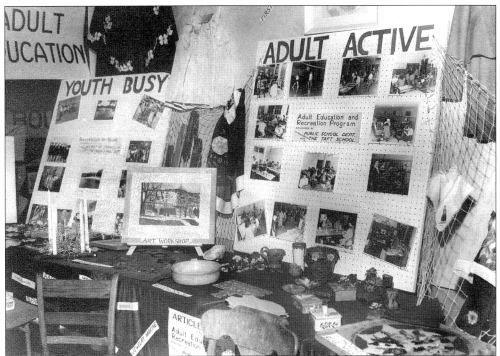

The Adult Education Association, working under the board of education, sponsored many evening classes for the residents. A fair was held and many items made by the students were displayed.

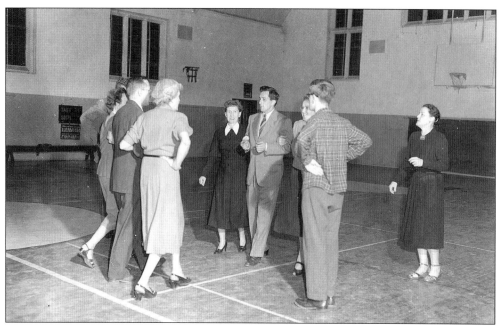

Taft School joined the Adult Education Association in some of its ventures. One of the many adult education classes in the 1950s was square dancing. Here, Isabelle Rowell is teaching square dancing at Taft School.

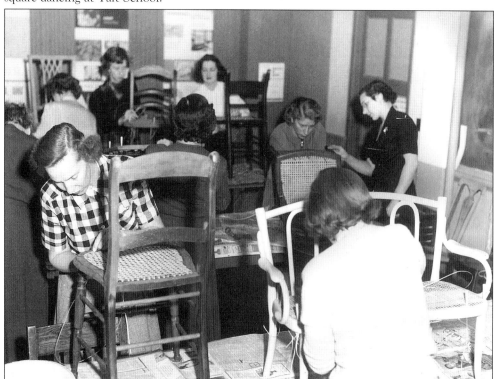

Another class that was held at Taft school was the chair-caning class. Many Watertown residents learned how restore old furniture under the tutorial of Ruth Getsinger.

Tommy:

Thought you would enjoy this book. I your birth place and youth home stead

Love

Joe & Cecile

P.S. Hope to see you soon

Five

HOMES OF YESTERYEAR

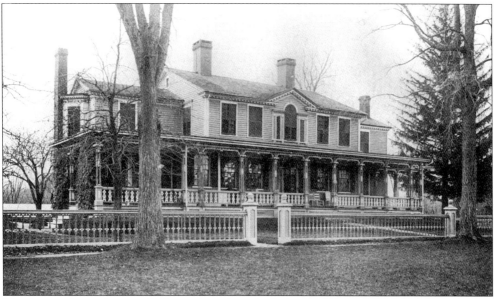

This house, dating from c. 1805, may have been built for Charles Merriman, a drummer boy of the American Revolution. Located on the green, it was owned by Alanson Warren Sr. of the Wheeler Wilson Sewing Machine Company and then by his son. John and Annie Buckingham purchased the house in 1879, and it stayed in the family until 1952, when S. McLean and Margaret Buckingham sold it to Dr. Glenn Jackson. In 2001, this house and about 80 other structures were placed on the National Register of Historic Places, and a Connecticut Historic District, including many of the same buildings, was established.

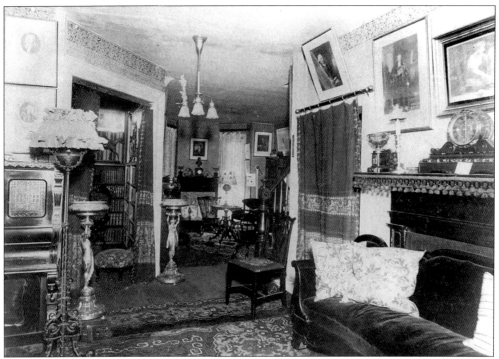

In 1936 and 1937, the Buckinghams gutted their house (seen also in the previous image). Porches were removed and wings reduced. There were two chimneys on the original house; in the 19th century, two more were added, but they were removed when the house was gutted. This image shows an area of the interior of the house before renovation.

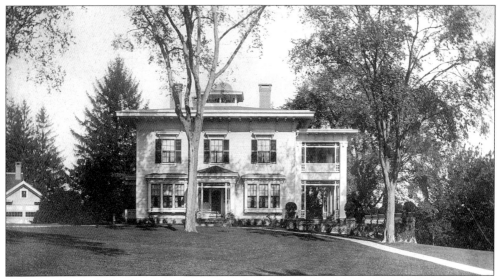

Amos Gridley built this house at the north end of the public park in 1849. In later years, it was the home of John Woodruff, the Dickermans, the Warrens, and James Woolson. In 1928, William J. Munson bequeathed the house and the land to the town in memory of his wife. The land is known as the Marian B. Munson Memorial Park, and the board of education offices are located in the house.

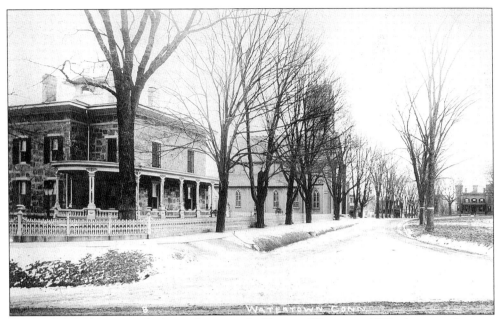

This Italianate house was built on the green for Truman Warren in 1851 of granite that was taken from a mine off Linkfield Road. He was an investor in the Wheeler Wilson Sewing Machine Company. A 19th-century iron fence imported from France surrounds the house. Charles and Alice Matoon owned it from 1898 to 1946.

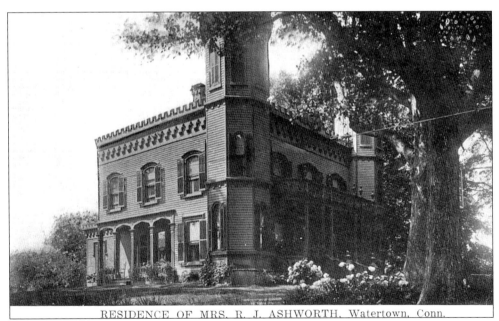

RESIDENCE OF MRS. R. J. ASHWORTH, Watertown, Conn.

In 1859, Charles Woodruff built this Victorian Gothic house at 7 Woodbury Road. Woodruff was an investor in the Wheeler Wilson Sewing Machine Company and in the Heminway and Bartlett Silk Company. The tall turrets were altered in the early 20th century. The Ashworth family lived here for more than 65 years.

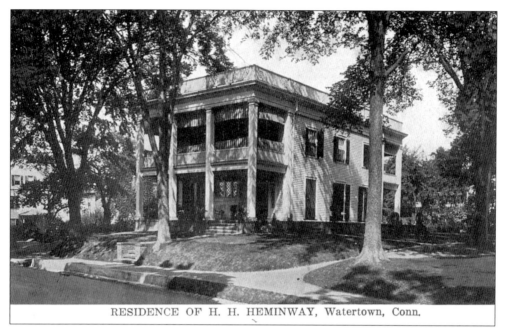

RESIDENCE OF H. H. HEMINWAY, Watertown, Conn.

This house was built in 1852 in the Italianate style by Nathaniel B. Wilson, the founder of Wheeler Wilson, the sewing machine manufacturers. When Harry Hemingway bought the house in 1914, he changed it to the current Colonial Revival style. Next door is an interesting brick carriage house that was built in 1863.

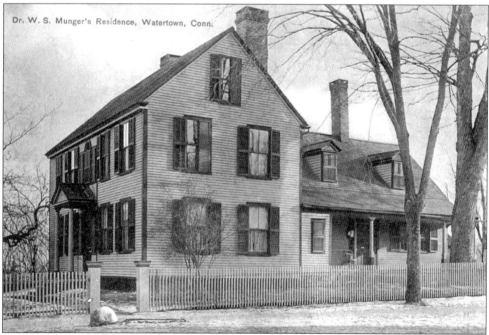

Dr. W. S. Munger's Residence, Watertown, Conn.

When local merchant Younglove Cutler had this house built on DeForest Street in 1783, it faced the drugstore. The DeForest family lived there until 1889, when Dr. Walter Munger purchased the house. In 1905, he turned the house so it faced the street. Marion Ottley then owned the house from 1927 to 1969.

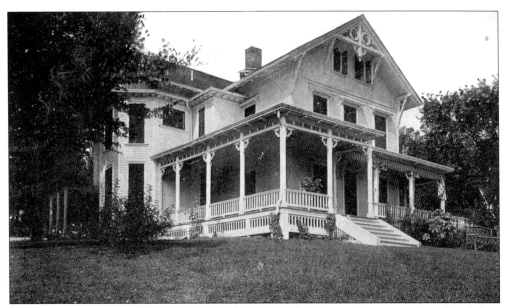

This house, of High Victorian Gothic style, was a gift to Mary Heminway from her father, Gen. Merrit Heminway. She married into the Merriman family, and Dr. Merrit Heminway Merriman was in residence there for many years.

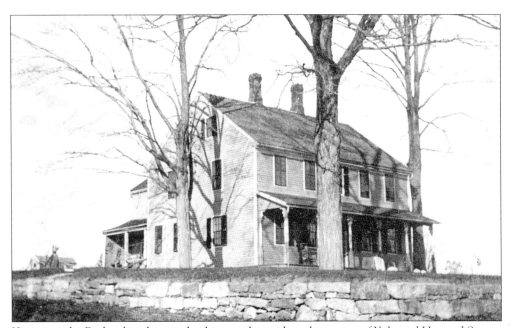

Known as the Richardson house, this house is located on the corner of Yale and Harvard Streets in Oakville. It was built in the 1730s and is one of the oldest houses in Watertown. It is also known as the Buckingham or Davis Homestead. There have been many changes made to this building over time.

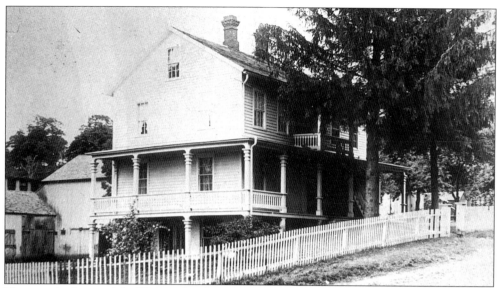

This was the home of the Warner family at the corner of Riverside Street and Hillside Avenue in Oakville. Russell Pope, a librarian at the Oakville library for many years, married one of the Warner girls. This house was moved up Hillside Avenue, and the Autoyre Company built on this corner. It is better remembered as the site of Winchester Electronics.

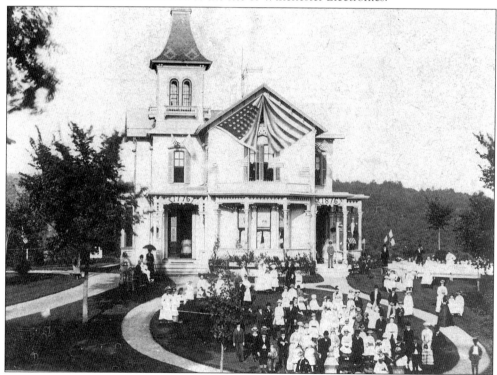

While Buel Heminway was having this house built on Main Street *c.* 1861, he and his wife lived in the old schoolhouse that was moved from the triangle. This photograph shows the house when it was decorated for the national centennial in 1876. A fire in 1961 severely damaged the house, and the structure blew up in the 1970s.

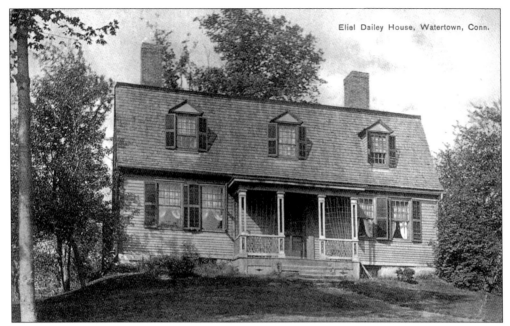

Known as the Dailey House, this Dutch Colonial was built on Main Street in 1782. Gen. Merrit Heminway moved here when he married, and it became the birthplace of some of his children. Eliel Dailey moved here in 1847. Dr. Glenn Jackson bought the house in 1949, restored the interior, but then purchased the Buckingham house on the green. The house was dismantled and moved to Cincinnati, Ohio.

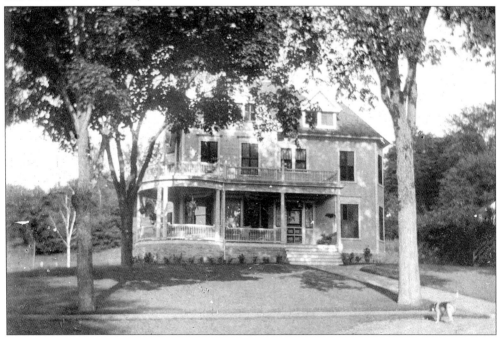

Merrit Heminway built homes for all of his children. This was for his son, Merrit Heminway Jr. The Rowlinson family resided here for many years. This structure was taken down, and St. John's Roman Catholic Church now occupies the spot.

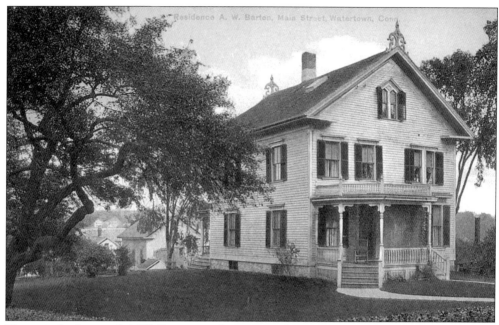

This was the home of A.W. Barton, at the corner of Main Street and Echo Lake Road. Dr. Harold Cleary moved it down the road in the 1950s and carried on his medical practice there. Thomaston Savings Bank erected a building on that site. The Barton house was taken down when the bank built a new structure.

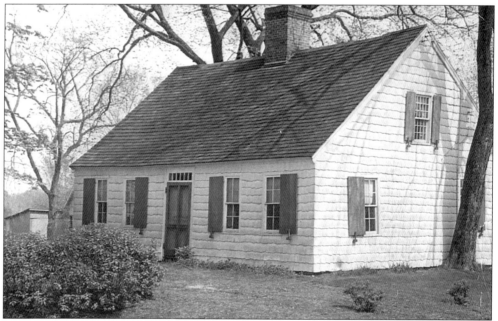

The Belden house is located at the intersection of Routes 63 and 73. Because a coin from 1735 was found over the door, it is presumed to be more than 260 years old. The Osborns, Thayers, and Beldings lived there, and at one time, it was a tearoom. After buying the house in 1947, Ozzie and Lavina Balunas added the Salt Box, a gift shop that is still in business. This is the oldest continuously lived-in house in town.

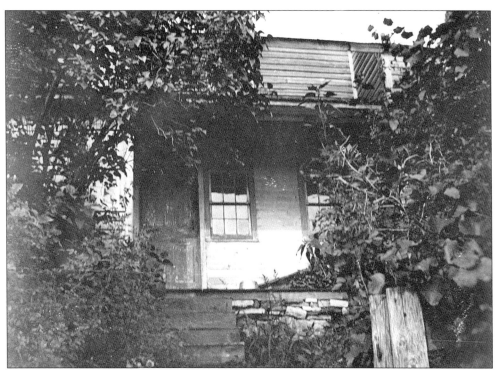

Mr. and Mrs. Wright Park purchased this house on Park Road *c.* 1858. Betty Park was clever with her fingers and fashioned a picture frame made of animal claws and toenails. She sent this to Pres. Abraham Lincoln and received a letter of thanks from him. She eventually opened a museum in her home where people could view the items she had made, as well as many stuffed wild animals.

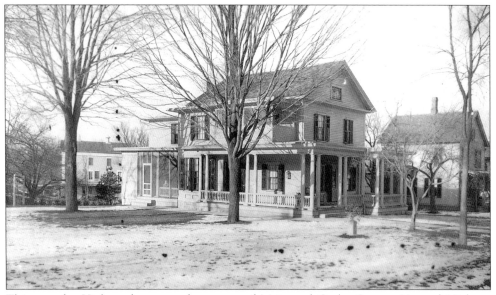

This was the Hickcox home, at the corner of Main and Cutler Streets. Howard Hickcox established Watertown's first funeral home, served as judge of probate for many years, and wrote most of the townspeople's wills in longhand for a fee of 50¢.

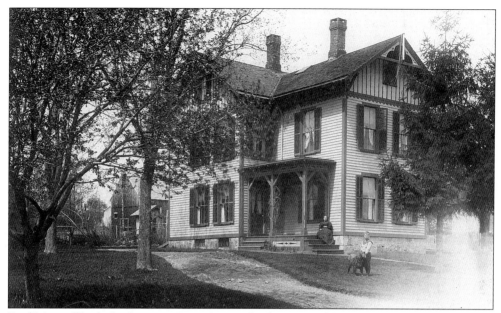

Emil Margraff built this house on Main Street after he returned from duty in the Civil War. The house was sold to Frank Campbell and was later moved to a parcel of land behind the house. It is still being used as a residence. The land was sold, and George's Market was built on that site. Margraff's son and grandson were dentists in town for many years.

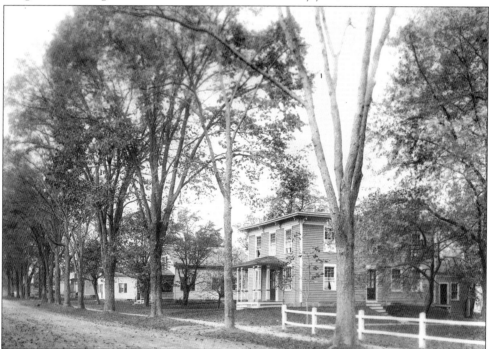

This photograph, made from a glass negative taken by Watertown photographer Harry Hard, shows Woodbury Road in the early 1900s. The houses are Bartlett, Brehan, Hard, Judson, and Welton. Taft School buildings have replaced most of these old homes, and one was moved to Wheeler Street.

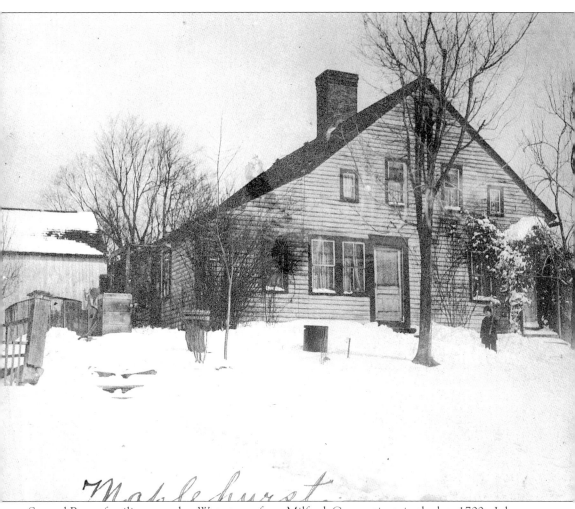

Maplehurst

Several Bryan families moved to Watertown from Milford, Connecticut, in the late 1700s. John Bryan built this house on the corner of Linkfield and Bryan Roads, and three generations have since lived here. When Boardman and Ruth Getsinger bought it in 1946, there was no electricity, indoor plumbing, or heating system. They brought the house into the 20th century. One interesting feature is the funeral door, seen at the far right in the picture. Funerals were always held in the home, and because of the center chimney, it was impossible to carry a casket into the house. This house has been placed on the National Register of Historic Places.

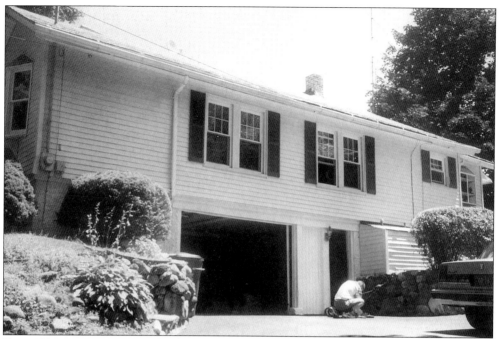

From 1909 to 1936, Sears Roebuck issued catalogs of houses. The price of each house was from $629 to $4,909, and the owner received plans and materials for a complete home. Many people in Watertown purchased these houses, and some are still occupied. The same family has lived in this Sears house at 29 Wilder Street for more than 40 years.

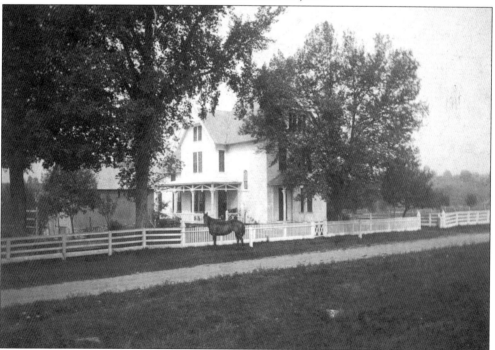

When the Camp family moved to Watertown, they purchased this farm on Buckingham Street in the Oakville section of town.

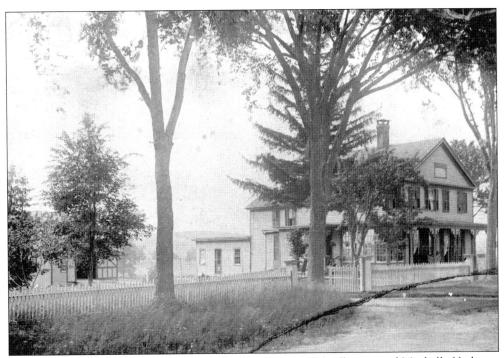

In the early 1940s, Fred Camp, who lived on the farm in Oakville, married Maybelle Hickcox. They purchased this house at the top of the hill on Middlebury Road. The fence has been removed, and there are now large white pillars, two stories high, across the front of the house.

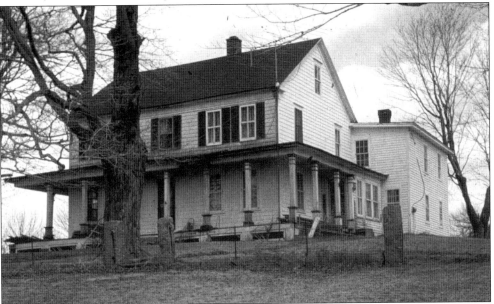

Joseph Garnsey came to Watertown from Milford, Connecticut, in 1730 and brought his slaves. He built a cabin in the area that is now called Guernseytown. At one time, there were 25 Garnsey families in the area. Native Americans chased Abijah Garnsey, and he fell down the stairs. His leg was amputated, and his father made two peg legs for him—one for weekdays and one for Sundays. These peg legs are at the museum.

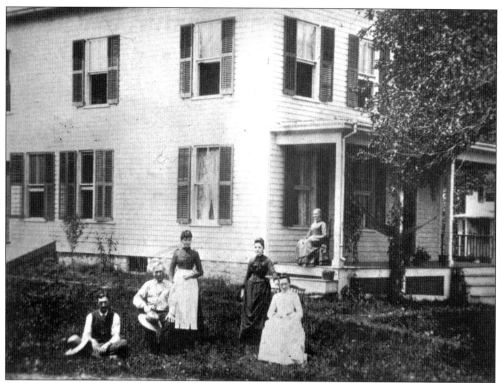

The Keilty family lived in this house on the corner of Woodbury Road and Hamilton Avenue in the early 1900s. They had a large family, and there are still many Keilty descendants in Watertown. The house was taken down in the 1950s.

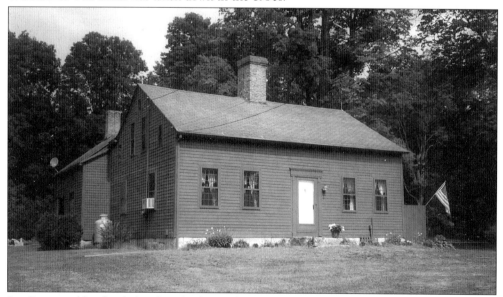

Joe Copes and his family lived in this house from 1926 to 1939. Copes immigrated from Italy in 1903. He raised pigs and collected kitchen and table scraps from Waterbury restaurants, worked at Chase Brass and Copper, and (in 1930) started Cope's Rubbish Removal. The company, now being run by the third and fourth generations, celebrated its 70th anniversary in 2000.

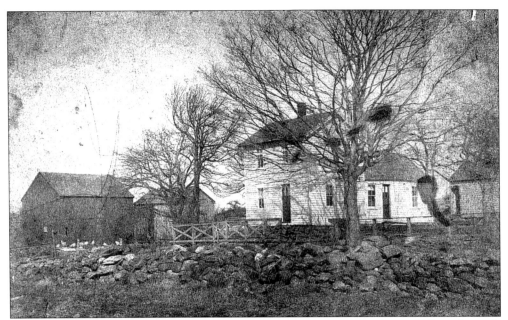

Edmund and Marcia (Fox) Monroe lived in this farmhouse on Nova Scotia Hill in the early 1900s. Edmund worked at the J.B. Woolson factory in the Greenville section of town. He died from a fall at the factory.

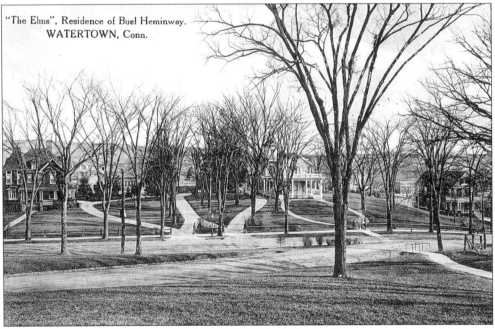

"The Elms", Residence of Buel Heminway.
WATERTOWN, Conn.

The house on the right, known as the Elms, was built by Buel Heminway. He built the one on the left for his daughter, who married a Mr. Klemke. That house is now the Methodist church parsonage.

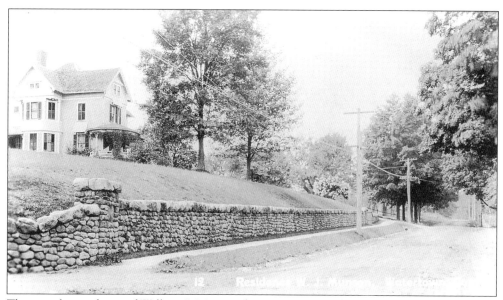

This was the residence of William J. Munson for many years in the early 1900s. It remains as a private residence today.

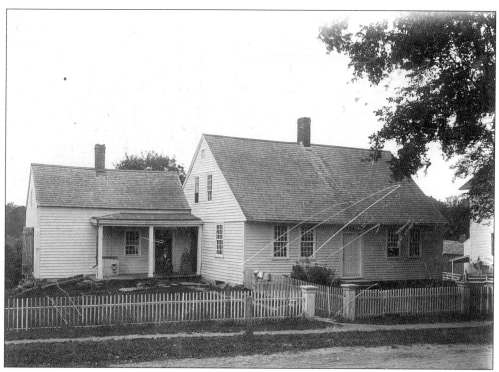

This was the home of a Mrs. Welton on Woorbury Road. Horace Taft, headmaster of Taft School, purchased this house in the 1930s. It was demolished, and a brick building was added to the Taft campus on that site.

Six
FRIENDS AND NEIGHBORS

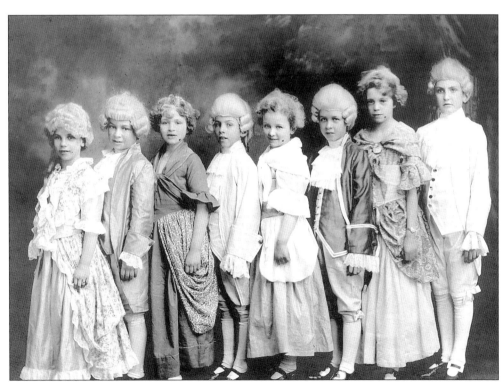

These children were ready to perform the minuet when this photograph was taken c. 1926. From left to right, they are Louise Campbell, John Sherwood, Selma Goldberg, Paul Foster, Maybelle Hickcox, Carl Berry, Cornelia Cook, and Francis Besancon. Leona Keilty, a longtime teacher in town, directed the performance.

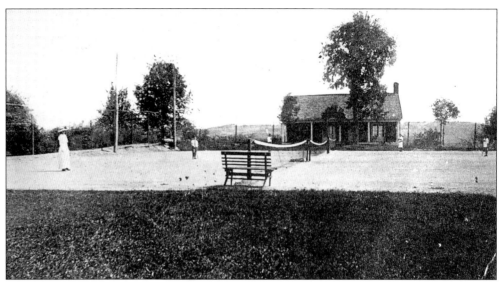

Residents of Watertown have been playing tennis at the Watertown Lawn Club since it was established in 1908. The name was changed to the Watertown Tennis Club in 1938. It is one of the oldest tennis clubs in the state. There are three well-kept clay courts that serve people from ages 5 to 85. Bill Tilden and Bobby Riggs, top men's singles players in the United States, participated in tournaments here in the 1950s.

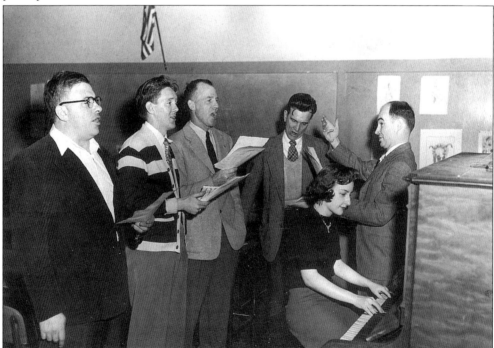

A barbershop quartet was one of the many groups in the Watertown Adult Education and Recreation Program in town in the 1940s. From left to right, under the direction of Carl Richmond, are Henry Stanko, Jimmy Duan, Royal Wheeler, and Jim Tignor practicing for their next program. Gwen Locke is at the piano. Carl Richmond was elementary music supervisor for the school department for many years.

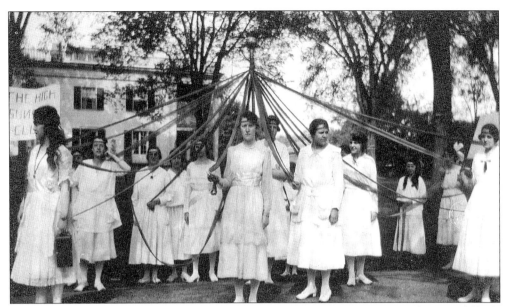

The Sunshine Club, a group of young women in town, is shown performing the very difficult maypole dance on the Christ Church green in the 1930s.

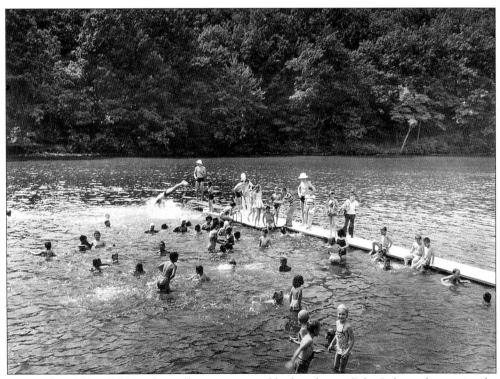

During the 1950s, children from all over town could take a bus to Echo Lake each morning for six weeks during the summer to attend the day camp as part of the recreation program. Activities included swimming lessons, crafts, and walks in the woods.

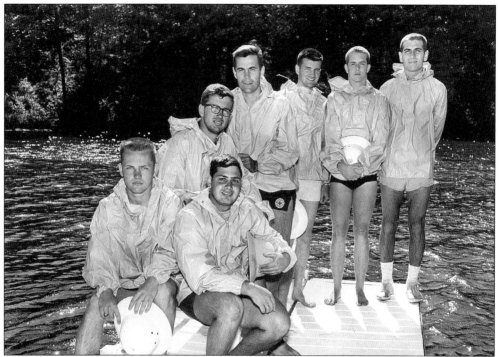

This group of lifeguards taught swimming at Echo Lake and Sylvan Lake to many children in Watertown during the 1950s. Many of the baby boomers learned to swim at these lakes.

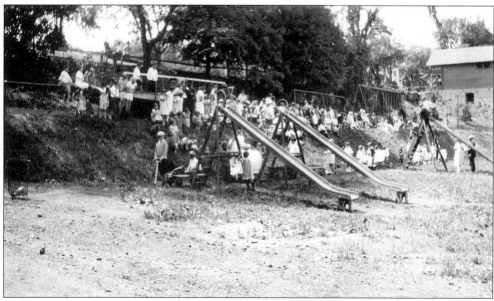

In 1920, the Watertown Civic Union installed this playground in a vacant lot next to the Community House. This photograph shows slides and swings. There was also a wading pool. Other activities included a wagon and carriage parade, costume show, baby show, and make-your-own-hat project. Madeline Flynn was playground director, and later Mary Kilbride was the director.

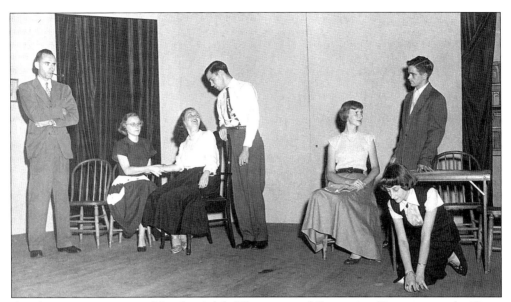

Another activity sponsored by the Adult Education and Recreation Program was the Town Players. Here is a group of young people who are rehearsing for their next production. Some of the people in the photograph are Carol Coon, Walter McGowan, Eleanor Smith, Nelson Corcoran, and J. Lewis.

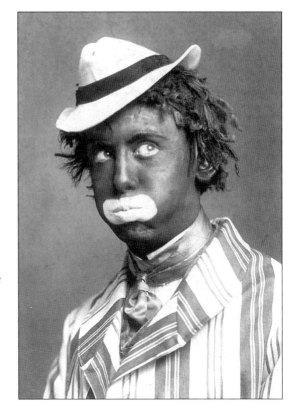

Sam Barlows's Minstrel was one show that was held on the second floor of the town hall. Music was by the Amphion Orchestra, and there was dancing after the performance. Advertisers in the April 9, 1917 program were the Watertown Trust; P.O. Drug; H.F. Atwood, dealer in groceries and meats; R.V. Magee, real estate and insurance; and J.F. McGowan, boots and shoes.

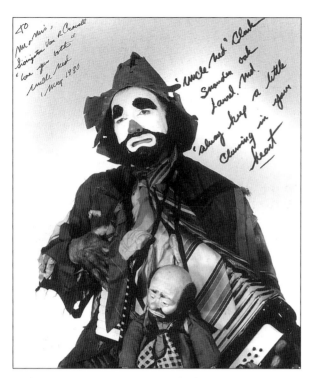

Watertown resident Ned Clark made a name for himself as a clown. Clark was one of the children who grew up at Aunt Grace's farm on Skilton Road. He joined the Marines and eventually worked in Washington, D.C. He became Uncle Ned the Hobo Clown and entertained people in nursing homes. The highlight of his career was when he met famous clown and comedian Red Skelton.

Titus Foote, a farmer, came to Watertown in 1817 and lived at the corner of Buckingham Street and Echo Lake Road. He had married three times, but all his wives had died. He had an Irish housekeeper, Hannah Donovan, who on May 9, 1861, went into his room and axed him to death. Found guilty of murder, she was sentenced to life in prison. She was pardoned six years later and then disappeared.

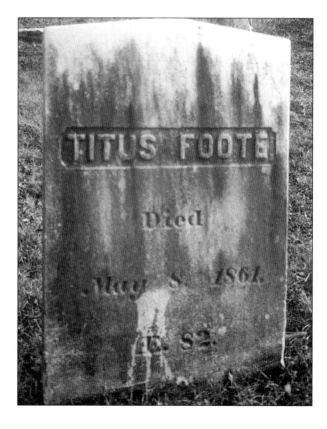

Jules Bourglay from Lyons, France, was down on his luck and came to America. As a self-imposed penance and wearing a heavy suit made of leather, he walked a 365-mile journey in 34 days every year for almost 30 years. He slept in caves and lean-tos, one of which can be found off Park Road. He died in one of his shelters in Ossining, New York, where he was found on March 24, 1889. He was buried in a nearby cemetery.

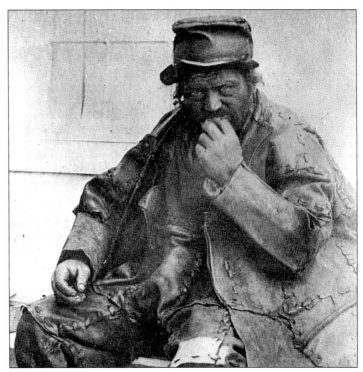

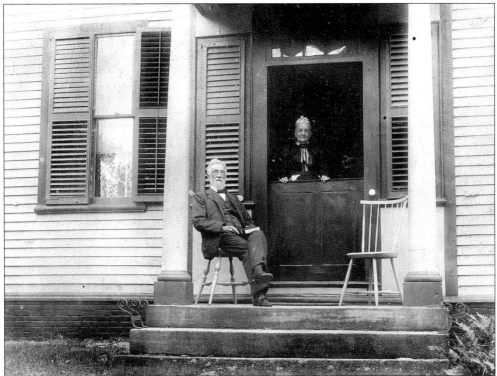

Dr. and Mrs. Munger are shown at their home on DeForest Street. Dr. Munger practiced medicine in town for many years.

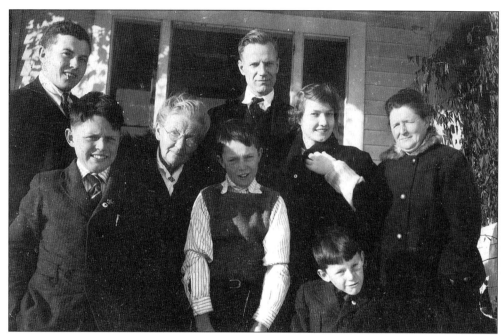

Faith Bassett was a descendent of the Garnseys who came from Milford in 1730 to settle what is now known as Guernseytown. Faith married Wilfred Bryan and raised their family on Grove Hill Road. This photograph from the early 1920s shows, from left to right: (front row) Harold, Richard, and William Bassett; (back row) Wilfred Bryan, Florence Lyman Bassett, John Bassett, Faith Basset Bryan, and Alice Hard Bassett.

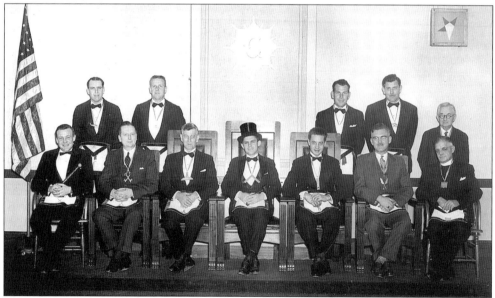

The first meeting of the Masonic Lodge was held in Watertown on December 22, 1790. Today, the lodge has about 200 members. This photograph shows the officers in 1948. They are, from left to right, as follows: (front row) George Chamberlin, Egdar Moberg, Charles Judd, Rondeau Allmand, Carl Weiss, John Barker, and Fred Wilcox; (back row) C. Edward Butterfield II, Art Carver, G. Floyd Cameron, Herman M. Turrel, and Peter N. Lund.

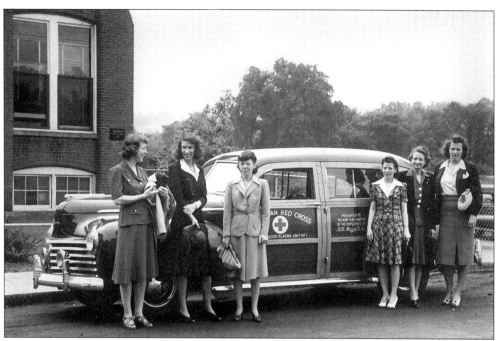

During World War II, the Red Cross bloodmobile visited the Princeton Knitting Mills in the old Heminway building on Echo Lake Road. This photograph shows some of the women who worked there. The Watertown Red Cross was an active organization in town for many years.

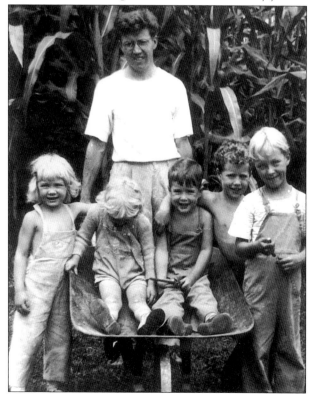

Bill Quigley and his family lived on Atwood Street in the 1950s. Here, he is giving Frances Smart (left) and Peter Quigley a ride through the cornfield in the wheelbarrow. The others are, from left to right, Elaine Smart, Bill Quigley, and Norman Smart.

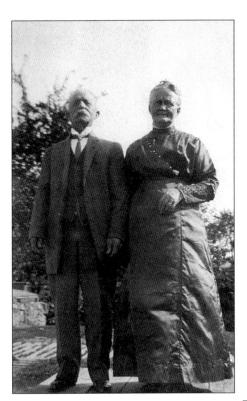

Samuel and Mary Hosking were married in 1891, and soon after, Samuel started a landscaping business on Porter Street that would continue for many years. This picture shows the Hoskings at an advanced age.

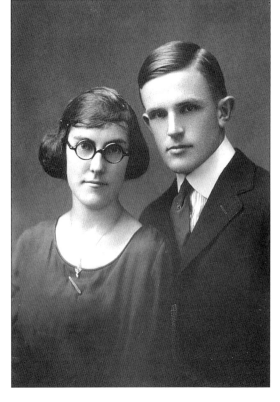

James Hosking, son of Samuel and Mary Hosking, married Sarah Johnson in 1922 and worked with his father in the landscape business. Sarah opened the Red Barn Gift Shop. Bill, son of James and Sarah, took over the business, and now his son, also named Bill, is the owner as it enters its second century in business.

Ashar Pritchard was born in 1785 and married Polly Hickcox *c.* 1804. He operated a blacksmith shop on Edgewood Avenue for many years with his son Benjamin and grandson George. Asher is the only War of 1812 veteran who is buried in the old cemetery. Other blacksmiths in town were John Kennedy, Peter Carley, Charles Griswold, Jay Morehouse, and Thomas Sutherland.

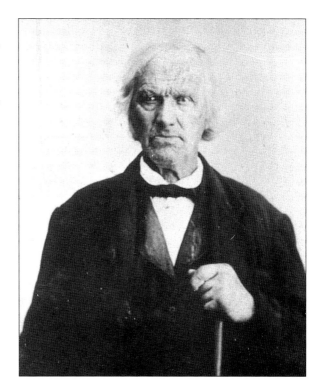

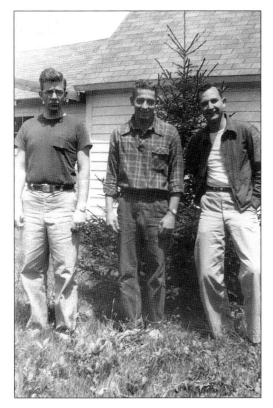

When this photograph was taken in the early 1950s, Livingston Crowell (left), Anthony Roberts (center), and Bernard Beauchamp (right) were teaching at Baldwin School. These men all became principals of schools in town. Crowell was principal of Judson School from 1956 to 1982. Roberts was principal of Heminway Park School, and Beauchamp retired after many years as principal of Baldwin School.

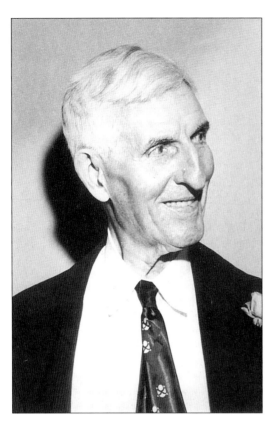

Fletcher Judson was president of the Watertown Bank and Trust Company. He was very active in town politics, especially in the education field. When a new school was constructed on Hamilton Avenue in 1956, it was named the Fletcher Jusdon School in his honor. He was also an accomplished horseman.

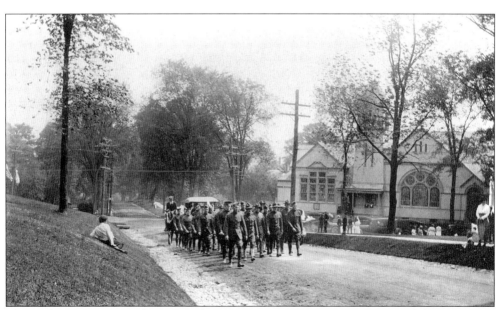

This is the 1918 Memorial Day parade as it comes up DeForest Street toward the town hall. World War I had not ended, so these men must be members of the Home Guard.

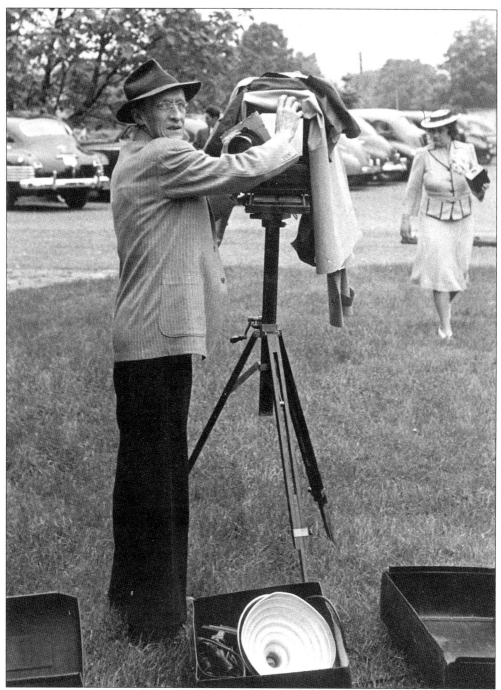

Harry Hard, seen here getting a pose ready for a photograph, was born in 1886 and moved to Watertown as a child. He studied photography under Lewis Bachrach of Boston and became a well-known professional photographer who served his town in many capacities. He held positions in local, state, and New England photographic societies. Hard loved the outdoors, fishing, hunting, and golf. He had his studio in Waterbury, and many engagement photographs of Watertown women were done by him.

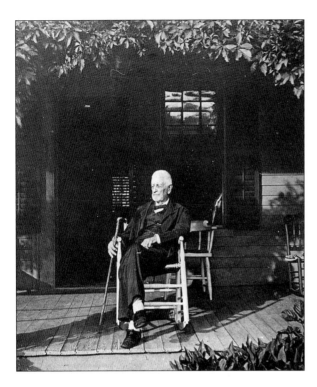

Leman Cutler was active in town politics and held many elected offices. He owned the land on which the depot was built in the 1870s. He is shown sitting on his porch in a photograph taken by Harry Hard.

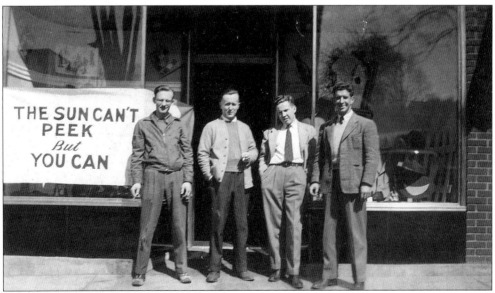

When Sullivan's Drug Store closed, Bill Quigley (who had operated the men's clothing store in the Byrnes building and then in the Pick Wick building) purchased the store and sold bicycles and skiing equipment. In front of the store are, from left to right, Bill Halliwell, Jim Hannon, Bill Quigley, and Nelson Ford.

The Goodwin family, who owned a chicken farm on Woodbury Road, posed for this photograph in the late 1920s. From left to right, they are as follows: (seated) Luella, Art, and Sterling; (standing) Dwight and Wesley. Sterling Goodwin was a mail carrier for the U.S. Postal Service for many years.

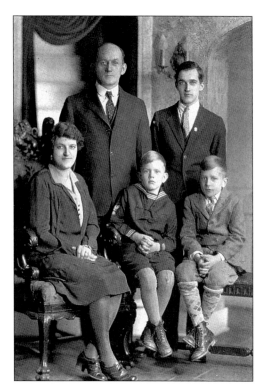

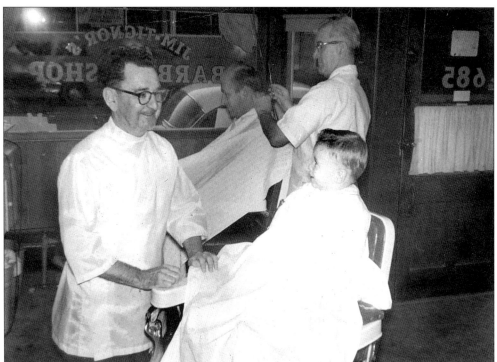

Joe Collins was a barber at 685 Main Street for over 50 years. Jim Tignor took over the shop, and here we see Collins in front and Tignor as they busily cared for the people in Watertown.

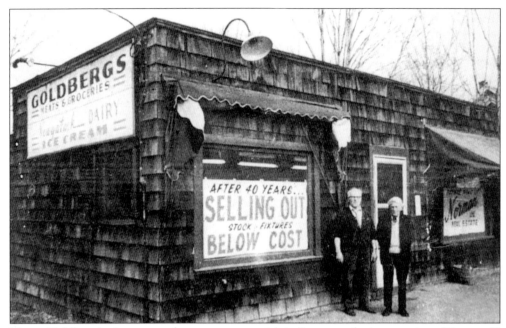

Morris Goldberg had a meat and grocery store on Main Street, at the intersection of Routes 63 and 73, for over 40 years. He performed a great service for the people in town because he was always open on Sunday. This was before the large grocery stores found that money could be made on Sunday.

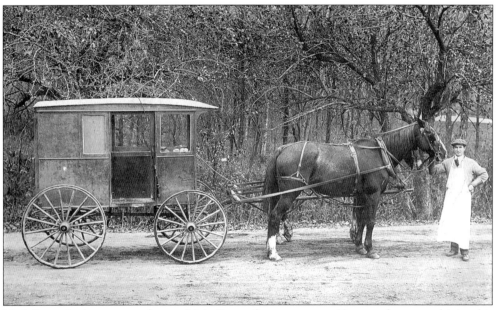

Herb Evans had a meat market on Main Street for many years. He was often seen driving his delivery wagon around town.

Edmund and Marcia (Fox) Monroe are shown wearing ribbons and badges at what is likely to be a convention. Edmund was a member of DeForest Commandery, United Order of the Golden Cross. They were both members of the Methodist church in Watertown.

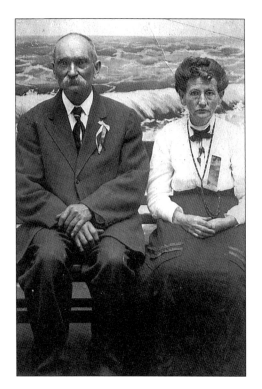

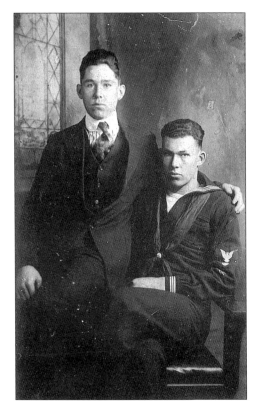

Clarence Cook (left) and wife, Rolene Monroe, lived on Hamilton Avenue. Cook had his own painting and paper-hanging business. He loved to hunt, trap, and fish, and he bought and sold animal furs. Clarence was in the army in World War I, and his brother Francis Cooke (right) was in the navy.

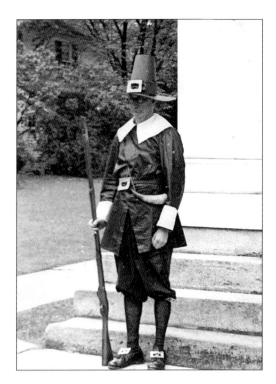

This is John Abbott when he attended the 200th anniversary of the First Congregational Church in 1939. Abbott was an accountant, and he could be seen frequently on Main Street, as he did the bookkeeping for many of the merchants in town.

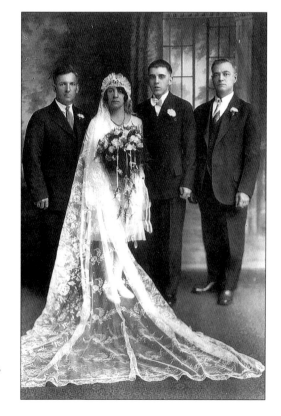

Rosalina Gelinas and Elzear Grenier were married on June 26, 1929, at the old St. John's Church on Main Street. Shown here, from left to right, are Adiren Gelinas, brother of the bride; Rosalina; Elzear; and Narcisse Grenier, father of the groom.

Seven
A FARMING COMMUNITY

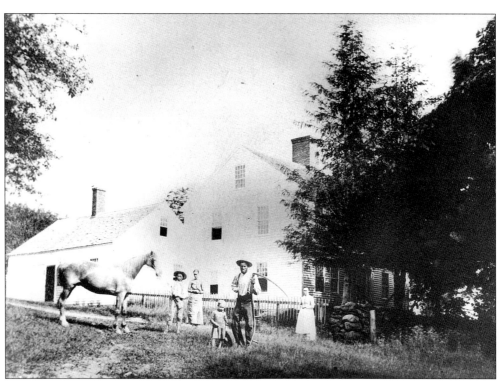

From its beginning, Watertown was a farming community. Merritt Skilton's farm was one of them. Rocks from a nearby ravine were used in the foundation of his house. Birdsey Skilton worked the farm for many years, and his sister Edith lived here. She died at the age of 104. Fearing that his only surviving son might be killed in the Revolutionary War, their ancestor, Dr. Henry Skilton, took his place so there would be a Skilton to carry on the family name.

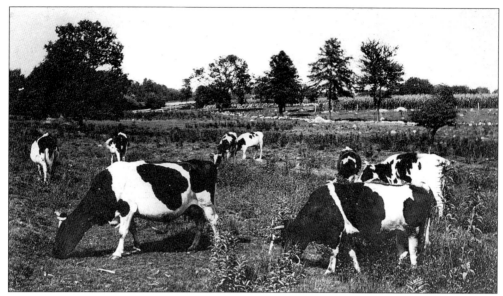

For many years, herds of cattle like these roamed the countryside. In 1870, William Munson built a large barn on Litchfield Road and purchased milking cows. He became Watertown's first dairy farmer. Most of the milk was sold in Waterbury. By 1896, more than 6,000 quarts were being delivered and, by 1906, 10,000 quarts. There have been more than 30 milk-producing farms here.

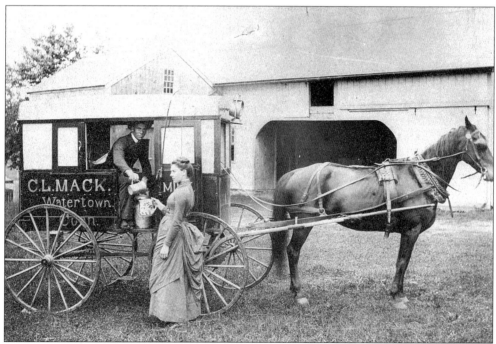

Calvin L. and Ellen Mack owned and operated a large farm in the Winnemaug section of Watertown. In this c. 1890 photograph, we see their son Frank E. Mack, daughter Lucy L. Mack, and their delivery wagon.

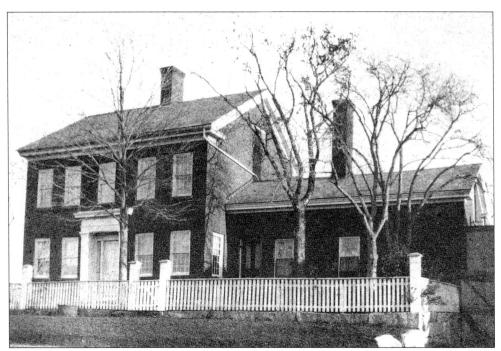

This was the house where the Mack family lived in the Winnemaug section of Watertown. Frederick Lynn purchased the farm c. 1900, and when he died in 1922, it was willed to his 13 children. His son Benjamin bought the house from his siblings. Robert, Benjamin's son, and his children, Nelson and Walter, run the farm and milk about 200 cows daily.

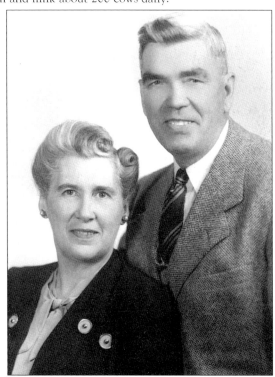

Benjamin Lynn and Rosetta Foster were married in 1914 and rented an apartment at Blazy's farm. Lynn worked for his father. They later moved to the old farmhouse, where they raised 10 children, 8 of whom are still living. Currently, there are only three dairy farms in Watertown.

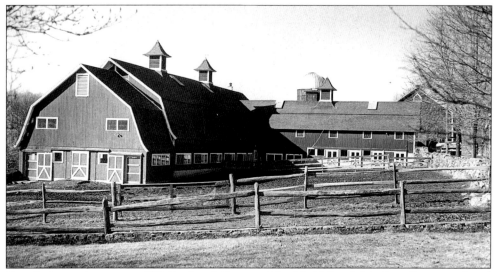

Sam Peck was the owner of Willowbrook Farm on Northfield Road. Much milk was produced here. James and Betty Christie purchased the farm and built a modern home there.

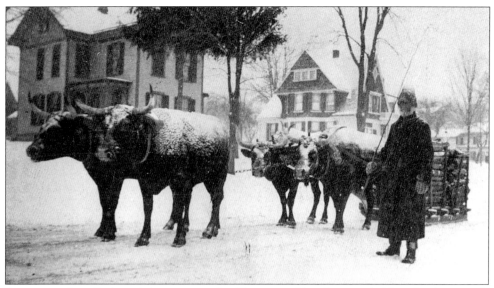

Every year, Sam Peck took his oxen to the Watertown Fair that was held at the fairgrounds opposite the Watertown Golf Club, and to many other fairs in Connecticut. He is shown here with two of his teams of oxen dragging a loaded wood shod.

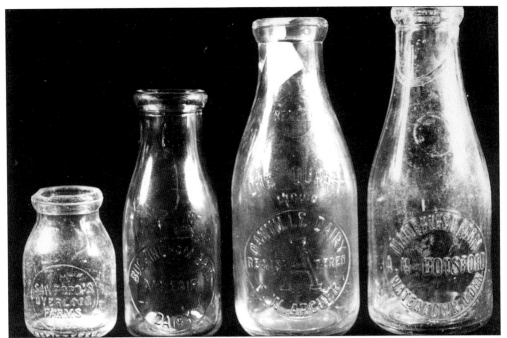

Milk was cooled in cans that were placed in the aerator through which cool spring water was continually running. The milk was then put into sterilized bottles and capped. The bottles were placed in a tank of spring water filled with chunks of ice. They remained in the tank, about one inch below the surface, until the milk was taken to market. These are bottles from Watertown farms.

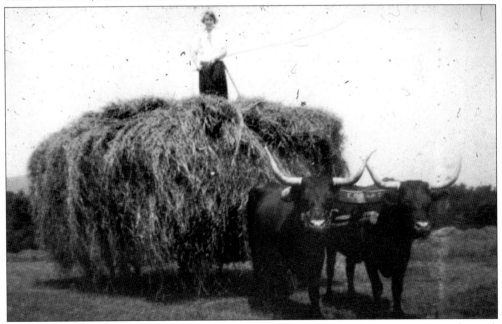

Gathering hay was a difficult task years ago. The hay was mowed, raked into windrows, heaped, and then pitched onto a wagon. Hazel Black is taking this wagonload of hay, drawn by oxen, to the barn, where it will be pitched in the haymow. The farmer's task is easier today because all hay is bailed.

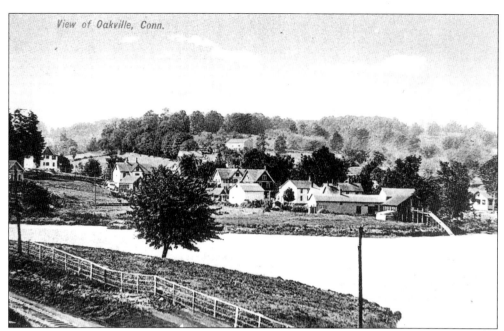

With all the dairy farms in Watertown, the farmers needed a way to keep the milk from spoiling before it went to market. In the winter, ice was cut from the many ponds in town, such as Pin Shop Pond in Oakville, shown here. In the background is the icehouse, and you can see the chute where the men pushed the ice inside.

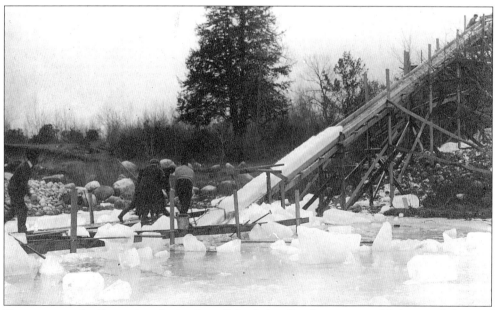

Here, men are busily cutting the ice from Echo Lake. Sawdust was sprinkled on each layer of ice to keep the blocks from freezing together. This lake became a recreation area, and many of the baby boomers recall learning to swim here and at Sylvan Lake.

An old steam boiler was placed here on Skilton Road 140 years ago to make a watering trough. The water runs through a pipe from a spring in the hill above. A farmer has stopped to give his team a drink after a long day in the hayfield. A team of thirsty horses can almost empty that container. Many people have used this trough when wells go dry in the summer.

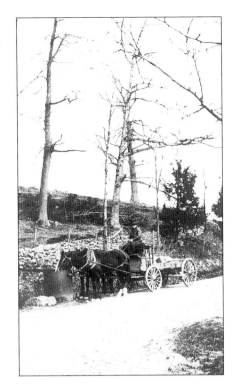

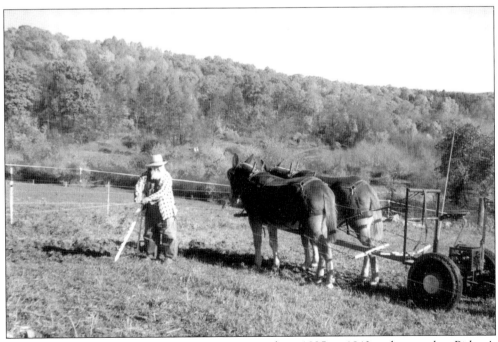

A mule train came through Watertown every year from 1825 to 1840 and stopped at Bishop's Tavern for the night. Farmers raised mules, and each fall men fanned out and bought them. As many as 300 grazed in the field and the drivers made merry. The next day, it was on to New Haven and the mules were shipped to the West Indies. These animals belonged to Henry Church.

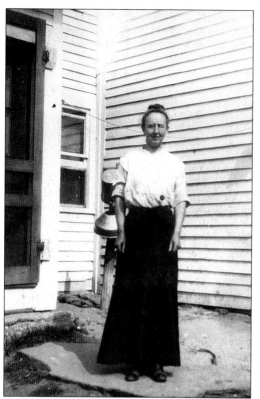

Will and Grace Foote had a farm on Skilton Road. Aunt Grace was an unusual, caring woman who took in the elderly and the young who had no home. She raised 14 children and cared for many others for short periods of time. Occasionally, there were as many as 18 people living in the old farmhouse. Aunt Grace never turned anyone away.

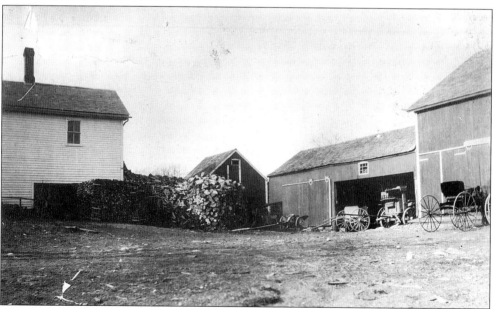

This photograph shows the horse barn, the carriage barn, and the woodshed on the Foote farm. Aunt Grace spent her entire life helping others. She lived in the 16-room farmhouse for 67 years, and most of the rooms were full all the time. She sent overcoats to the Bowery Missions, rolled bandages for lepers, and sent toys and dolls to underprivileged children. A nearby pond was dedicated to her in 1954.

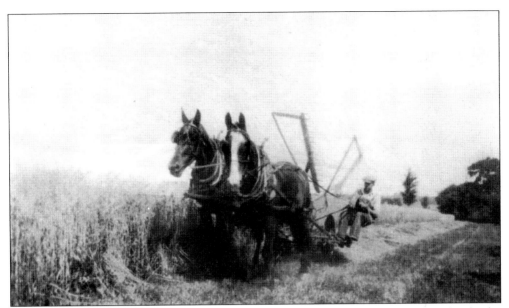

The Wheeler family owned two farms on Guernseytown Road. This is Howard Wheeler mowing hay the old-fashioned way. The Wheelers had many cows that had to be milked morning and night. The milk was cooled and taken to town each morning.

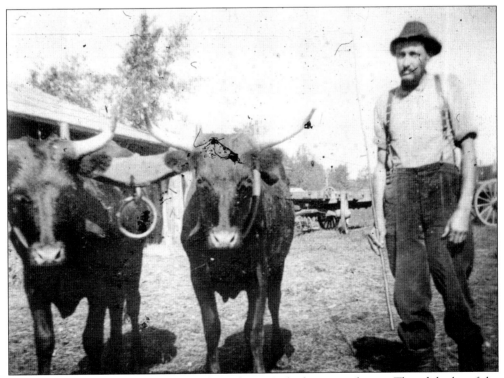

Elnathan Black, like many farmers in the early 1900s, had a team of oxen. They did a lot of the heavy work on the farm, and he took them to the Watertown Fair and other fairs in Connecticut.

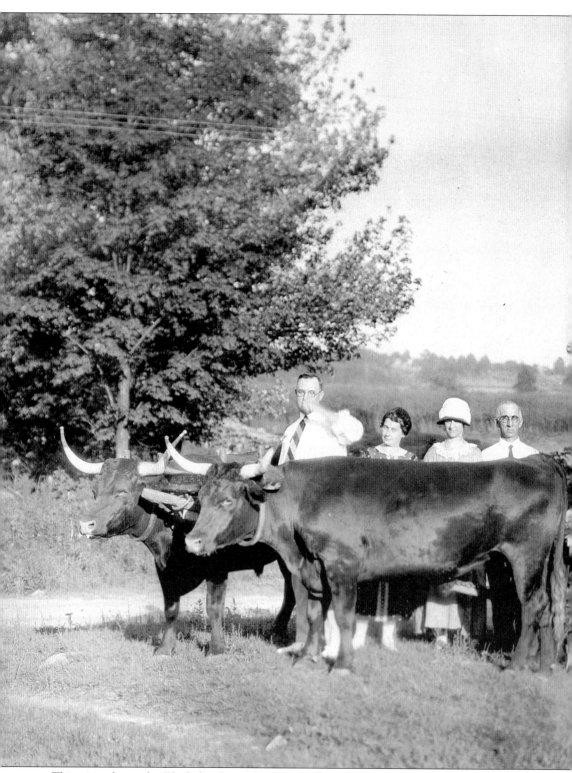

This view shows the Black family celebrating the Fourth of July with a picnic at Elnathan's

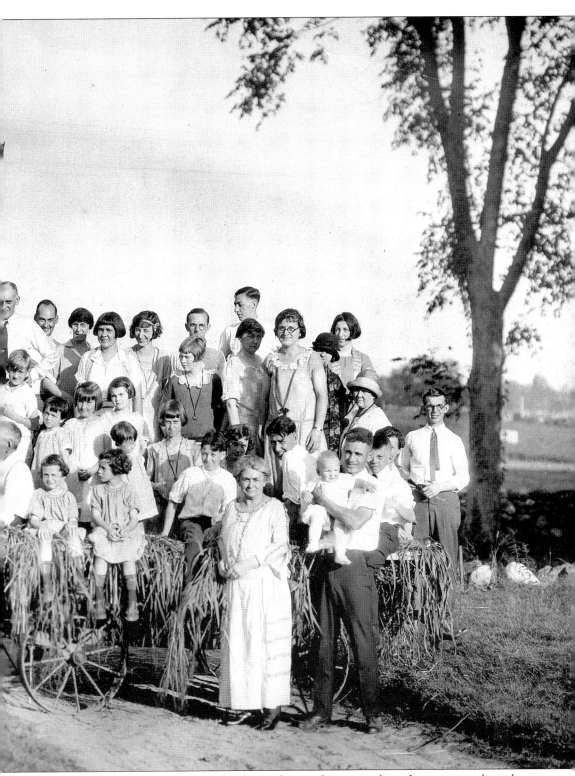

house on Northfield Road *c.* 1924. Elnathan is driving the oxen, taking the group on a hayride.

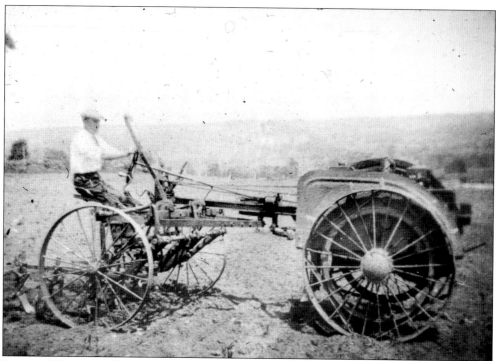

Raymond Black had the first tractor in Watertown. He is seen here working the Scoville farm on Litchfield Road.

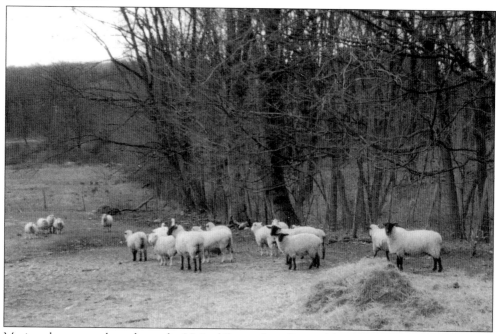

Merino sheep were brought to the United States from Spain. Many Watertown farmers raised sheep. Lack of fences made branding necessary, and the town clerk devised a different earmark for each farmer. Records at the town hall show all of the branding marks and to whom each was assigned. Between 1795 and 1865, more than 450 sheep herds were registered.

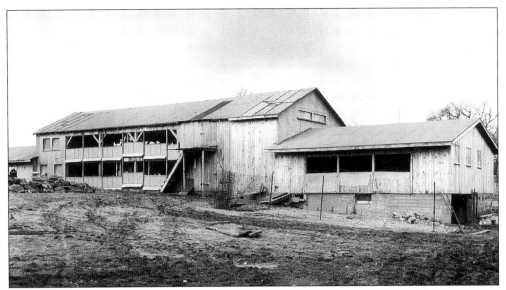

Out on Woodbury Road, Dwight Goodwin raised chickens. This is a two-story laying house where 1,200 white leghorns made their home. There was cackling going on all day as each hen told the world that she had laid an egg. Watertown photographer Harry Hard took this photograph in 1928.

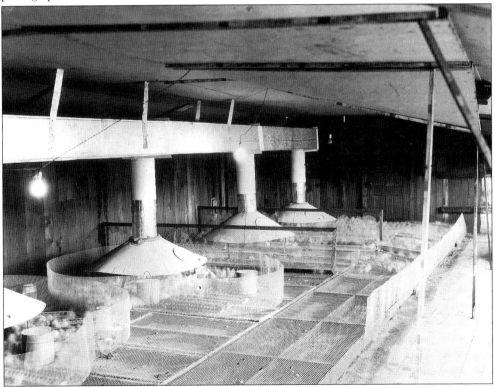

Another Harry Hard photograph shows the brooder house at Goodwin's chicken farm, which could accommodate 4,000 baby chicks. They would run around under the hot-air mechanical mothers. Thermometers regulated the heat day and night.

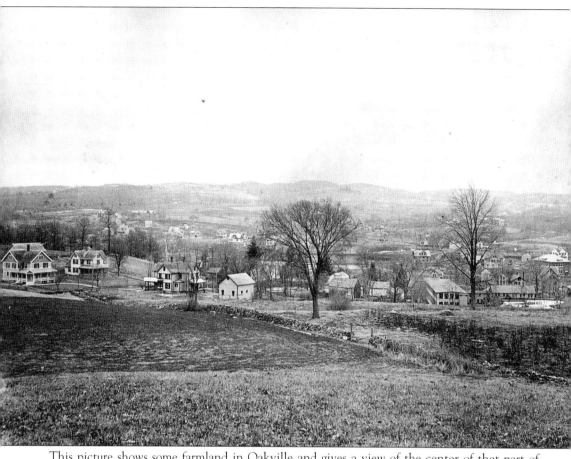

This picture shows some farmland in Oakville and gives a view of the center of that part of town. Oakville was once called Littlebury. European immigrants came to Waterbury and then to Oakville, where they could buy a plot of ground on which to build a house. In 1903, they auctioned off building lots, and many people were on hand to purchase one. On the far right in this photograph is South School when there were only eight rooms. By the tree on the right is the Seymour Smith and Sons factory, and behind the tree in the center of the picture is Pin Shop Pond.

Eight
AROUND THE TOWN

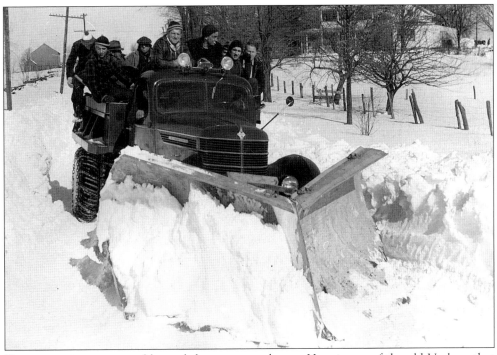

Years ago, winters were colder and the snow was deeper. Here is one of the old V-plows that were used on the rural roads. One of the Wheeler houses on Guernseytown Road can be seen to the right in this February 1940 photograph. Many times, the snow was so deep that the men had to shovel before the plow could be used.

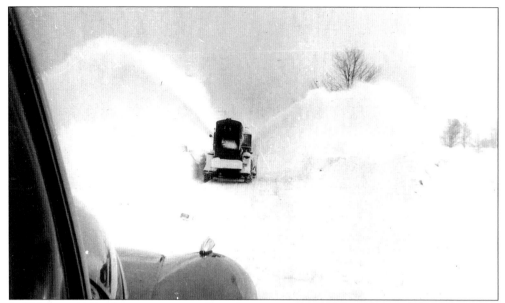

In February 1948, the snow was so deep the town rented a snowblower from the town of Goshen. This photograph shows the blower working its way down the flat on Skilton Road, just off Guernseytown Road.

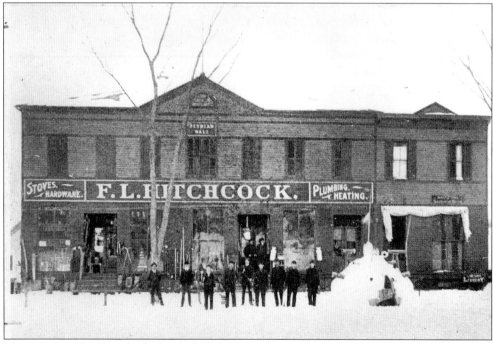

The Knights of Pythias built this hall and used the upper floor for meetings. They rented out the lower floor to F.L. Hitchcock, who carried on a plumbing and heating business. Snow shovels were left in the pile of snow until someone came to purchase one. The first floor is still a store, and there are apartments on the upper floor. The first telephone office was located in this building.

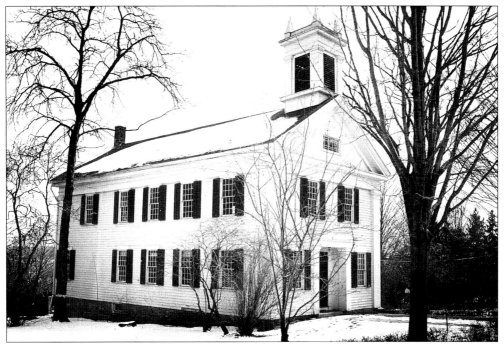

In 1846, the parishioners of Christ Church built the Academy. It was used as a private and public school, Watertown's first high school, first library, church parish hall, for Red Cross meetings, sewing groups, boy and girl scouts, plays, and recitals. The members of the Christ Church are currently renovating the building.

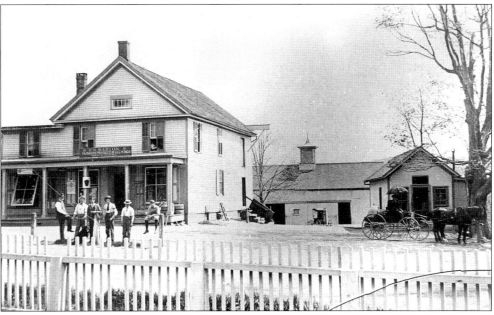

The F.N. Barton Store, at the corner of Woodbury Road and Sunset Avenue, was in business in the latter part of the 1800s. The library was moved from the Academy building to the second floor of this building in the mid-1860s. Nancy Bronson had been appointed librarian and continued in that capacity for more than 38 years.

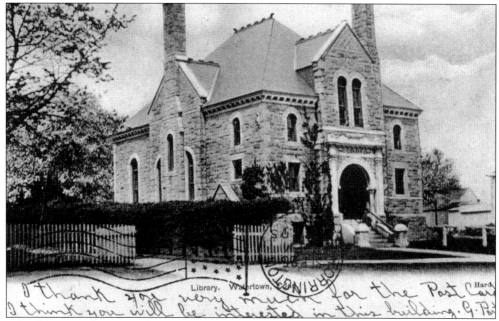

Library. Watertown, Conn. ... I thank you very much for the Post Car[d]... I think you will be interested in this building. G. Pa...

After being on the upper floor of the Academy for a year, Watertown's library moved to the second floor of Barton's Store. Dr. John DeForest and his brother Benjamin were generous contributors to the library. Dr. DeForest gave $10,000 and Benjamin gave $15,000. After his death, Dr. DeForest left another $10,000 in his will. This building was used from 1881 until the new library was built in 1958, and it now belongs to Taft School.

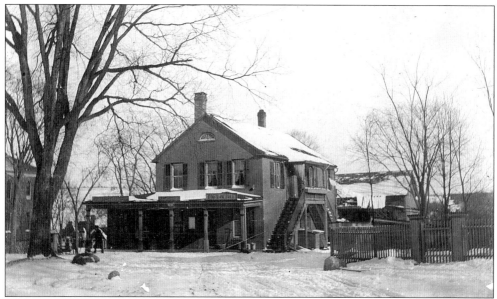

There has been a store at this site since 1730. Several additions have been made, and through the years, it has been known as the Trading Post, Starr and Clark, Southworth's, Randall's, the Post Office Drugstore, and the Post Office Drug and Health Complex. The post office was in this building until a new structure was erected next door.

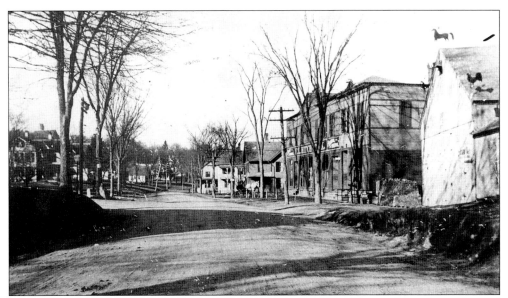

Main Street was still a dirt road when this photograph was taken in the early 1900s, and telephone polls had arms and insulators. The building on the right was Dayton's theater. Next to that is Pythian Hall. The houses in the center gave way to stores in later years.

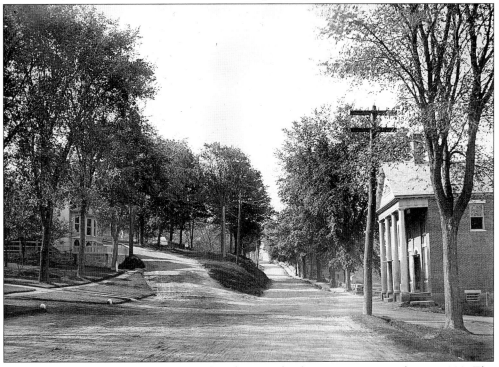

Many changes have taken place since this photograph of Main Street was taken c. 1900. The brick building, now a restaurant, looks the same, but the road has been widened and is now paved. Academy Hill has been closed, and there is a high decorative wall to hold the bank. Gen. Merrit Hemingway's house is on the left at the foot of Academy Hill. All of the lovely elms have disappeared.

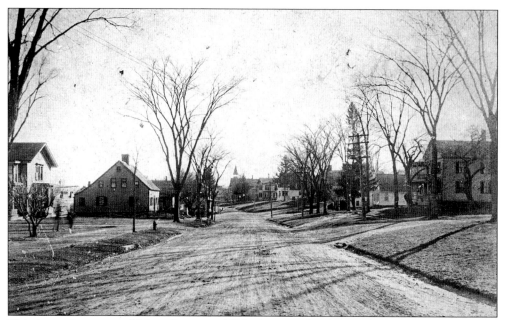

This is another view of Main Street in 1905, showing the dirt road. It was taken from the intersection of Echo Lake Road looking south. The saltbox on the left now has a storefront, and the rest of the buildings are gone. In the center is the steeple of the first St. John's Church.

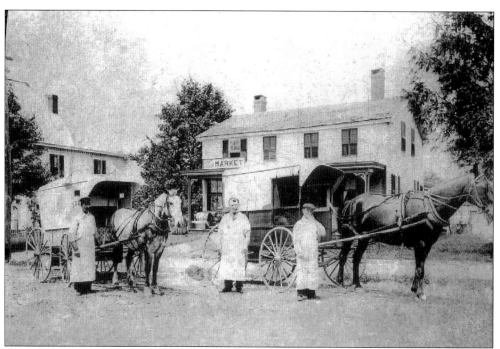

Five generations of the Labonne family have been offering the people of Watertown meats, fish, poultry, produce, and groceries since the early 1900s. George opened his first store in Jewett City and moved to Watertown, where someone from each generation has continued the business.

A plaque was placed on this elm tree behind the town hall by the Daughters of the American Revolution to commemorate the first unfurling of the Stars and Stripes in Watertown at the close of the War of 1812. Many people attended this event.

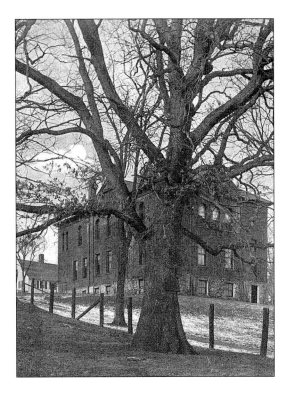

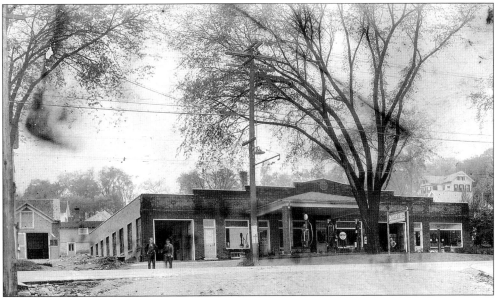

After Ellen McCleary's Elmhurst Hotel burned in 1930, Art Johnson built this garage opposite Depot Street. This 1927 photograph shows the building before bowling alleys were added on the second floor. Raymond West, who ran Cities Service Station, bought this station in 1945 and became a Chevrolet dealer. When he moved his business to Woodbury, Brooke's Drugs took over this location.

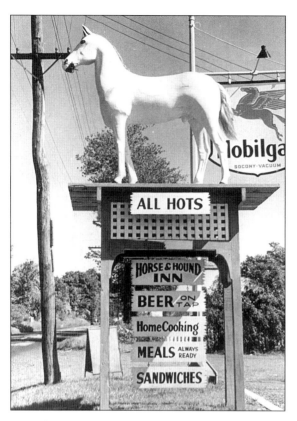

In the 1930s and 1940s, the Horse and Hound Inn was located on Thomaston Road at the corner of Buckingham Street, where the Westbury Room is located today. It attracted people from near and far. White Horse Whiskey was being advertised, as was Mobilgas, with the sign picturing the flying red horse. This photograph was taken by Jack DeLano of Watertown in September 1940.

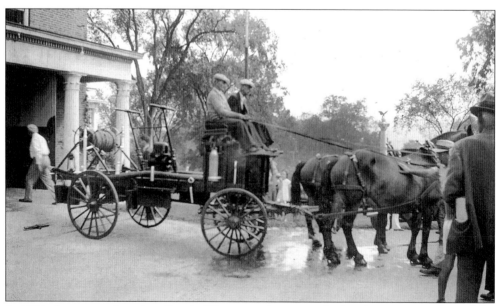

In 1894, there were six serious fires in Watertown in one week. A volunteer group formed the first fire department. This was the town's first fire truck, which was kept in Buel Heminway's barn on Main Street. After the new town hall was built, the Gridley building became the firehouse. The horses were stabled at Brahen's barn on Woodbury Road.

Amos Gridley built this store in 1846, replacing Garrit Smith's wooden structure. The post office was here in 1853. In 1864, it became the town hall, then the firehouse from 1896 to 1951, also Masonic Hall, a kindergarten, and a barbershop. Since 1953, the lower floor has housed the Watertown Fire District, and the Watertown Historical Society Museum has been on the second floor since 1969.

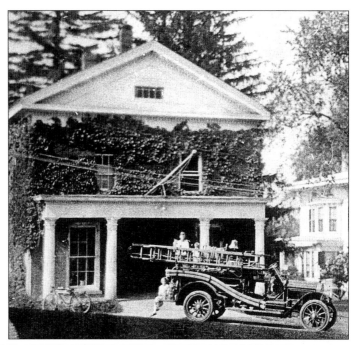

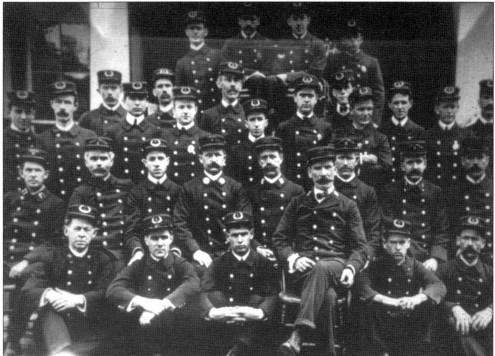

Fire alarm boxes were installed in town in 1896. In 1904, 10 years after the Watertown Fire Department was formed, the men of the department gathered on the steps of the town hall for this photograph. The members had waterproof coats and hats in 1908. This volunteer department celebrated their 100th anniversary in 1994, and they are still protecting the community today.

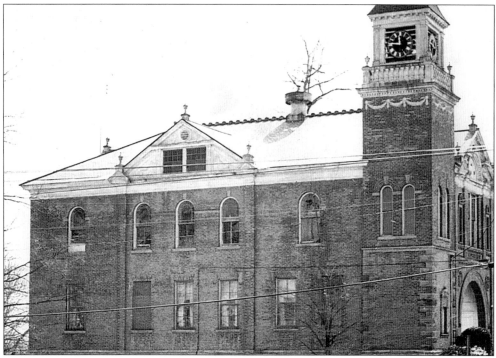

This town hall was built in 1894 when the hall across the street became inadequate. The offices were on the first floor, and the upper floor was used for town meetings, plays, and graduations. The basement housed the police department and the jail. The upper floor was condemned many years ago. Many town offices are now located in the town hall annex and at the Depot Mall.

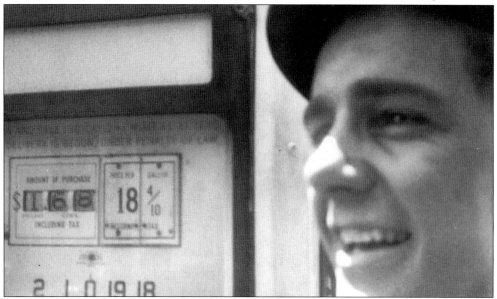

One of the employees at West's Cities Service Station was pleased that in 1940 gas was selling for 18⁴/₁₀¢ per gallon. A few years before, the price was $1 for eight gallons. Raymond West ran this station at the corner of Main and French Streets for approximately nine years until Carlton Lockhart took over the station in 1945.

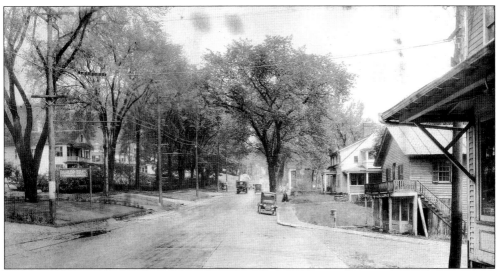

This is a 1927 view at the intersection of Main and Depot Streets. Johnson's garage is advertising Dunlop Tires at the far left. The pillars of the bank building can be seen in the center, and the building on the right with the stairs and porch is where Dan Sullivan opened his first drugstore in 1899.

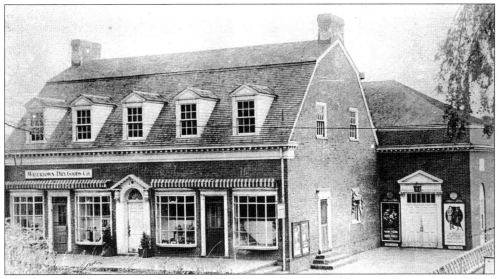

The Community House was erected in 1917 by a group of public-spirited citizens who had formed the Civic Union. This organization sponsored many civic groups: the Visiting Nurses, Americanization, Dramatics, Girls Club, Boy Scouts, and Girl Scouts. They also worked to improve parks, schools, and playgrounds. This has been the movie theater in town for many years.

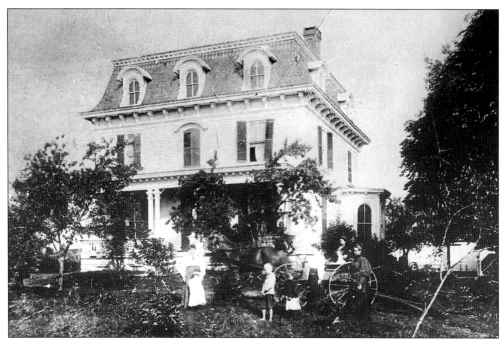

This building was erected on Hamilton Avenue in the mid-19th century and served as a sanatorium where the wealthy could come for fresh air. In 1914, Dr. Charles Jackson ran an On the Hill Resort. In 1930, it became McFingle's Inn. After World War II, it was made into apartment for returning servicemen and their families.

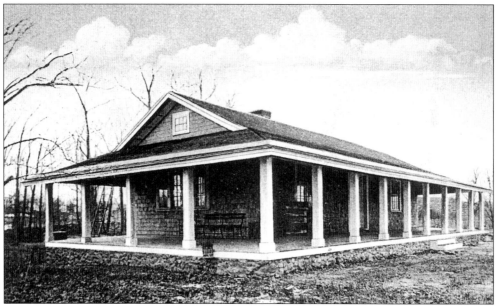

This bungalow was on the McFingle's Inn property and used when Dr. Jackson ran his sanatorium. On October 6, 1925, David Woodward invited 50 dinner guests to the bungalow and a nonprofit philanthropic organization, the Watertown Foundation, was formed. The organization continues to thrive, and it gives scholarships and grants to Watertown residents and organizations.

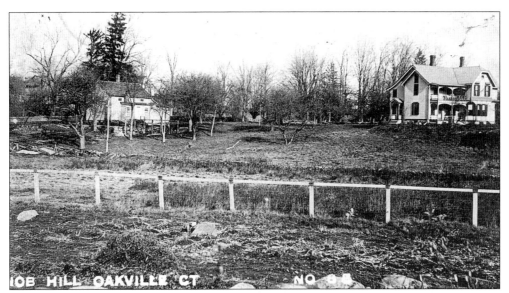

Legend tells us that someone who lived in the area of St. Mary Magdalen School traveled to California in the 1890s. He returned to Oakville and named the area Knob Hill. A photograph, showing Harry Hard's house on the right, was taken and this postcard was made c. 1900.

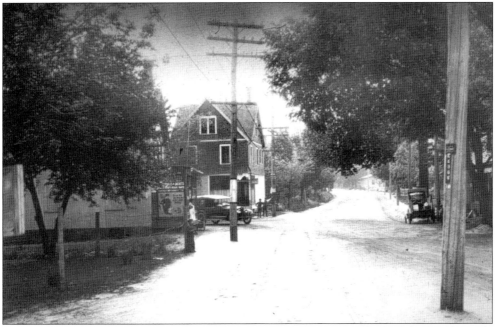

Main Street in Oakville has definitely changed since this photograph was taken in the early 1900s. The road is not paved, and trolley tracks can be seen in the foreground. A vintage automobile can be seen entering Main Street from Davis Street. The telephone pole seems to be in the center of the highway.

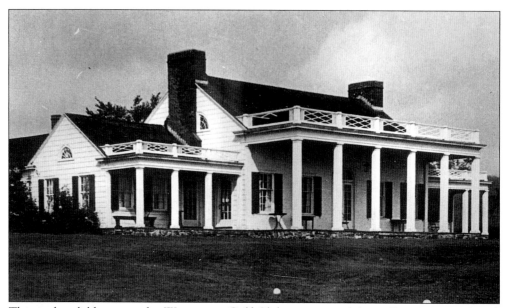

This is the clubhouse at the Watertown Golf Club, a private club on Guernseytown Road, founded more than 75 years ago. A large dining room has been added since this photograph was taken. This was the only club in town for many years, but Crestwood Park Golf Club, a public course, is now available to residents and people from out of town.

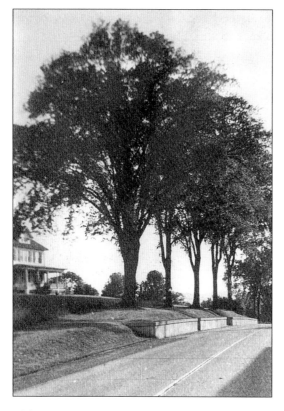

This photograph, taken in the 1930s, shows the Stockman house on Woodbury Road. When Dutch elm disease hit Watertown, most of the trees died and these were no exception. The wall was made higher when the road was widened.

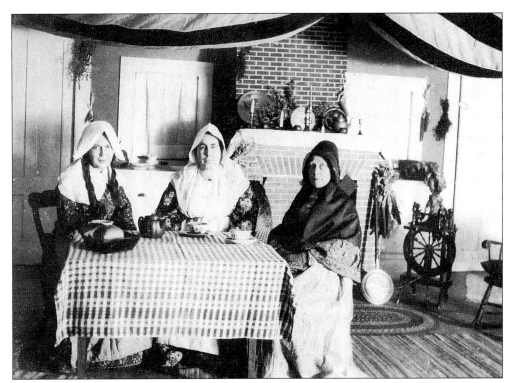

Pictured from left to right are Marjorie (Black) Barlow, Bertha (Atwood) Hudson, and Helen (Scoville) Smith at a fair sponsored by the Watertown Historical Society in the 1940s. People demonstrated weaving, quilting, chair caning, candle making, and many other crafts here.

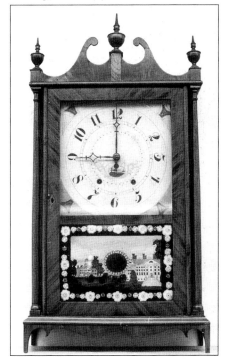

This is one of the old Bishop and Bradley clocks that was made in the factory on Cherry Avenue. The factory used waterpower from the dam at the top of the hill. This clock can be seen at the Watertown Historical Society Museum.

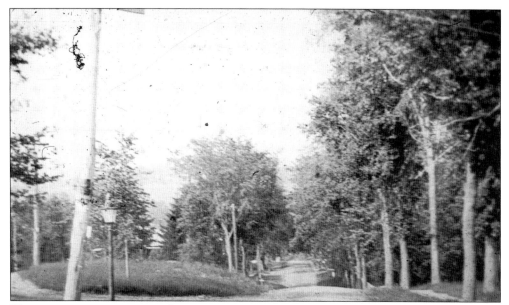

This interesting picture was taken on DeForest Street, in front of the town hall looking east c. 1900. The road to the left would take you the Congregational church. There is a gaslight on a pole on the left of the picture.

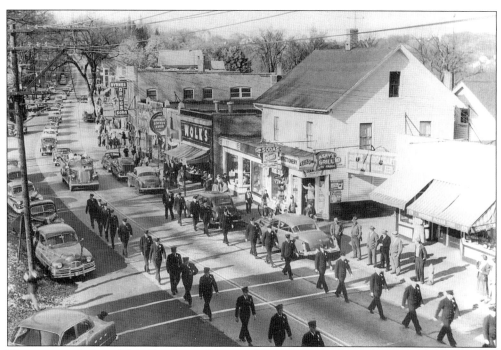

Firemen march down Main Street in a Memorial Day parade in the early 1940s. Stores familiar to many are Leo's Confectionary, Wolk's Department Store, Ashy's Grill, Butterley's Coffee Shop, and Byrnes Drug Store.